ENDORSEMENTS

Ken has been an invaluable partner in guiding my family's investments for over two decades. As an independent money manager, he skillfully utilizes alternate vehicles and unique strategies—options not commonly accessible to traditional wirehouse advisors. Ken's ability to safeguard capital in challenging economic times is unparalleled. A dedicated student of macro trends and broader market conditions, he offers a distinctive perspective that ensures a truly effective approach to protecting wealth. His expertise and insights have made him an essential part of our financial journey.

**— MIKE MASAREK, INSURANCE EXECUTIVE
IN COMPLEX LIFE INSURANCE PLANNING
VALUED CLIENT FOR OVER 20 YEARS**

I have known Ken for over 25 years. We discussed the risks in the markets back in 2007 and he correctly navigated the 2008 bear market and protected our capital. Ken and his team are always looking to protect our wealth, but not afraid to be aggressive when the timing is right. He definitely thinks outside the box including catching Bitcoin early.

**— ALAN RUTNER, PRESIDENT, PURITY WHOLESALE GROCERS
VALUED CLIENT FOR OVER 15 YEARS**

Ken's knack for protecting capital, even when the market is in decline, is remarkable. His perceptive market insights, as well as his unwavering dedication to our financial well-being, have distinguished him from the pack. With Ken, we have not only found a professional who knows the markets through and through but also a trusted partner who consistently places our interests first.

—JAMES ZENDA, PRESIDENT, ZENDA LLC
VALUED CLIENT FOR OVER 10 YEARS

Ken is keenly aware of risks in portfolio management and protecting capital. As in the bear markets of 2001 and 2008, he and his team have taken great care to protect our assets and grow our wealth.

— BILL BURLEY, RETIRED VP & GM, CITRIX,
EXECUTIVE CONSULTANT AT BURLEY CONSULTING
VALUED CLIENT FOR OVER 25 YEARS

BEYOND WALL STREET

7 PRINCIPLES OF RISK MANAGEMENT & WEALTH PRESERVATION

KEN ARNOLD

Printed in the United States of America

Limit of Liability/Disclaimer of Warranty:
The author provides no warranties on the accuracy or completeness of this book and disclaims any implied warranties. Seek advice from a professional tailored to your situation. The author and publisher disclaim liability for any financial or commercial damages arising from the use of this book.

Financial Disclaimer:
This book is for informational purposes and does not substitute personal or professional financial advice. While the author is a licensed financial advisor, the content provided herein does not constitute financial, investment, or legal advice. It is crucial to consult with a qualified financial professional before making any financial decisions or investments. Financial decisions involve inherent risks, and the author shall not be held liable for any financial or investment decisions made by readers based on the information presented in this book. All financial decisions are the sole responsibility of the reader and any consequences, whether positive or negative, arising from these decisions are not the author's responsibility. Readers are encouraged to conduct their research, seek advice from qualified financial experts, and carefully consider their financial goals, risk tolerance, and individual circumstances before making any financial decisions.

Paperback ISBN # 978-1-7329322-5-8
Hardcover ISBN # 978-1-7329322-6-5
eBook ISBN # 978-1-7329322-7-2

Library of Congress Control Number: 2023924097

Design by Sarah Siegand
Production by Jennasis & Associates

www.ken-arnold.com

DEDICATION

To the next generation of investors.
May they learn from our mistakes.

CONTENTS

FOREWORD

When Ken asked me to write a foreword for his book, I was thankful he chose to write about investing rather than one of his other passions like martial arts—a subject that is not in my area of expertise.

All jokes aside, while I might struggle to find as many accolades for those pursuits, as an investor and money manager, I am happy to share that Ken's 40-plus years of experience have made him exceptional at risk management. Through some very dramatic markets, Ken and his clients have survived and thrived.

Ken's focus—and the focus of Everglades Global Advisors—is risk-adjusted returns. Not since very early in our careers have we seen an investment climate like this, with rising interest rates and soaring inflation. Risk management is the key to investing in today's landscape. It's all about making a good return on investment while avoiding big hits; not biting off more than you can chew, and so on.

Ken's approach to risk management is different from others. He's seen a lot of dramatic ups and downs in his investing career, and he's come out of it alive, with his client's money intact. There are many major banks, investors, money managers, etc., who can't say the same, unfortunately.

It's not just about experience and expertise, though. At Everglades, our main focus is managing risk. We're not investing prodigies, masters of business, or even psychics. We've simply found a strategy that works for us and our clients and allows us to toe the line of risk and reward. Sometimes we lose, just like everyone else, but the difference is that we make sure our losses do not handicap us or our clients.

I recommend you take Ken's advice to heart. You might have to search for the advice—it's hidden amid stories about Bernie Madoff and Bitcoin—but it's there. Rationality and risk management are crucial to preserving wealth in these tumultuous times.

Peter E. Lacey
Chief Investment Officer
Managing Member of Everglades Global Advisors LLC

INTRODUCTION

"Don't gamble! Take all your savings and buy some good stock and hold it till it goes up, then sell it. If it don't go up, don't buy it."

— Will Rogers

You're in the right place.

No matter who you are or where you come from, you have made the right choice by picking up this book.

Why?

Because investing is for everyone. Actually, let me revise that: everyone should be an investor.

Investing helps you grow wealth passively, beat inflation, plan for the future, keep yourself afloat in a bad year, and retire comfortably.

This book can help you do all of that—and more—whether you're a seasoned investor or just a beginner.

Investing is a practice, just like riding a bike or learning to paint. Anyone can pick up a paintbrush, and investing is the same—anyone can do it, regardless of the money in their bank account. Everyone has a different style, too. Some are risk-averse and others are willing to gamble on riskier bets. Some are into investing in start-ups, while others hedge their bets with a more stable investment like gold or works of art.

Some people have a knack for it, others must learn how to become the next Picasso. My belief is that you can always hone your skills, learn from others, and think about things differently.

No matter how you want to invest or what you want to achieve, I wrote this book to review the basics of investing, point out some of the things you might not be thinking about, and help you avoid the (almost inevitable) pitfalls of Wall Street. I've seen too many good investors, with good instincts, get swept up in the euphoria of Wall Street, all because they didn't have any principles or vision to ground them.

Most of all, I have some grave concerns about the future that you should protect yourself against. I'm no whistleblower—these are not new issues—but they are things that are not discussed in Washington or on Wall Street. It is my hope that the chapters of this book illuminate a path toward effective risk management and wealth preservation.

Through working with clients for over four decades—decades which have seen massive highs and lows in the financial world—I have distilled seven guiding principles that I want you to have at your disposal.

Let's get started!

CHAPTER 1

A COVENANT BROKEN

"I, however, place economy among the first and most important republican virtues, and public debt as the greatest of the dangers to be feared."

— Thomas Jefferson

There's a big problem that might make it impossible for you to invest, and nobody's talking about it.

The United States government has a financial covenant with its citizens written into the Constitution, to maintain the stability of the economy, provide essential public goods and services, protect citizens' rights and property, and ensure a fair and just taxation system.

Despite this covenant, there have been instances—such as economic instability, political instability, natural disasters, or other unforeseen events—in which the government has failed to fulfill its financial obligations to its citizens, leading to broken promises and significant economic consequences. Such a breach can be dire for the American people, especially those who are investors.

A government or central bank may break their promises

or agreements to maintain a stable and predictable monetary policy. This can occur when they engage in actions that undermine the credibility of their monetary policy—such as excessive money printing or fiscal stimulus without appropriate measures to manage inflation.

For example, if a central bank promises to maintain low inflation rates, but then engages in a policy of excessively low interest rates or quantitative easing, it may be seen as breaking its covenant with the public. These actions can lead to a loss of confidence in the central bank, which can ultimately result in higher inflation as individuals and businesses begin to anticipate rising prices and demand higher wages and prices for their goods and services.

It's well known and understood that a stable, healthy currency is vital to the productivity of society. Unstable currency—whether due to inflation, high exchange rates, high interest rates, or weak imports/exports—make life more expensive for those living and working in areas of the world that have an unstable currency. Lack of stability stymies growth, scares away foreign investors, causes widespread generational poverty, and stifles innovation.

When governments devalue their currency—purposefully or otherwise—the issues that arise from that decision are not only economical. Psychologically, the more unstable the currency, the less the public trusts the status quo and the more likely they are to attempt to preserve as much of their wealth as they can with severely limited options.

Here's our problem in the simplest terms: at the time of writing (September 2023), we have a national debt of $32.17 trillion dollars in the United States.[1] At the current rate of spending, we're set to hit over $40 trillion by 2028.[2] This number does not include current and future obligations of national programs like Social Security and Medicare, but if you factor those in, the debt will hit well over $150 trillion.

In 2000, the national debt was $5.7 trillion. In 2008—just eight years later—the debt had doubled to $10 trillion. In fifteen years, we've gone from $10 trillion to nearly $40 trillion— an increase of nearly 300%. Our debt has outpaced gross domestic product (GDP) for several years already, but pandemic-era spending caused us to reach an all-time high of 134.8% of GDP.[3]

Our country's high and rising debt matters because it devalues our currency, threatening our economic future and society as a whole.[4]

Thanks largely to international conflicts, unforeseen circumstances, and seriously irresponsible monetary policy-making, our national debt has ballooned out of control.

To pay off the national debt as it stands today, each taxpayer would be obligated to pay $206,000 upfront, right now.[5]

But they're not knocking on our doors just yet. So, even if you have $206,000 to spend, current runaway inflation will likely make your obligation (or your grandchildren's obligation) be much higher and paid with dollars that are worth significantly less.

There are solutions to this, but it seems Washington would rather sit and argue about it, ignore it altogether, or make it worse.

For example, keeping interest rates historically low for years coupled with major supply chain shutdowns during the pandemic caused inflation to spike from 1.4% in 2020 to 6.4% in the last months of 2022 and early 2023.[6]

To attempt to curb inflation, the government is raising interest rates and printing more money. In fact, in the last 20 years we've printed more money than ever before. More money in circulation can help lower interest rates, giving more people the opportunity to borrow, buy, and invest. However, if the money supply grows beyond the demand for goods and services, it will actually increase inflation instead.

International conflicts change the landscape of our economy, too. With the war between Russia and Ukraine, sanctions on Russian oil have driven energy prices—specifically crude oil and other raw materials—through the roof. Russia supplied roughly 3% of the world's oil production, causing a serious price hike at the pump when it was removed from the market.[7]

This is a frustrating problem, but not really a new one.

I began working on Wall Street after I graduated from college in the early 80s. I went to school for economics and ended up becoming a CPA, but it didn't take long for me to realize that I hated accounting. I wanted to help people preserve their wealth, and the tax code generally is not very good at that.

Plus, at the time the United States was still in the middle of what is now known as The Great Inflation. Spanning nearly 20 years, The Great Inflation was characterized by unprecedented inflation rates—over 14% in 1980—and interest rates rising to almost 20%.

It was an incredibly challenging time and the looming risk of losing carefully accumulated savings was genuine as each dollar dwindled in value. Some products became too expensive and simply were out of reach for many Americans. The standard of living in this country declined, as did the trust and confidence many had in the government. International conflicts caused oil embargoes that quadrupled the price of gas. It took a brutal recession—with the unemployment rate at more than 10%—to kill The Great Inflation. It was the first time we'd seen an economy like this.

Several things caused The Great Inflation, but one of the primary reasons was the massive surge of newly-printed money in the economy coupled with artificially low interest rates. Coming off the spending spree of the

Vietnam War, our national debt ballooned as we tried to avoid a recession.

Sound familiar?

For the most part, these are avoidable problems. Obviously international conflict is out of the average American's hands, but the risks of keeping interest rates low and printing money excessively are well known.

All of this to say, your ability to invest—effectively keeping your head above water when times get tough—is seriously limited when monetary policy makes a mockery of your wallet.

After years of working on Wall Street I realized something—the financial industry wasn't helping people. Sure, we made money, but at what cost? I saw firsthand how the system favored the wealthy, leaving everyday people struggling to make ends meet. I wanted to help people keep the money they earned and that's how I ultimately landed where I am today.

I co-founded Everglades Parkland Advisors in 2004 with the vision of helping people invest their money effectively, teaching them how to manage risk, and advising them as times get tough. Over the past 18 years, we've been lucky enough to achieve that vision. This is not something we take lightly. We're simultaneously humbled and honored that our clients choose us to help them, and we take their trust extremely seriously.

However, an investment firm can only do so much. Preserving one's wealth becomes challenging when the government fails to handle its own finances responsibly.

See, there are two important factors that determine the behavior of an economy. First is the fiscal policy, or the governmental body managing taxes and budget. Second is the monetary policy, which is generally the responsibility of a central bank. Monetary policy determines the printing of money and regulates the money supply, as well as monitors the economy for signs of excessive heating or cooling. Monetary policy also allows the central bank to enact regulations (such as interest rates) to help stabilize the economy as needed.

The issue is, the left hand doesn't know what the right is doing and vice versa. The two hands need to work together to support the economy—not separately, and certainly not against each other. But our government is big and sluggish, and the problem in recent years has mainly been that the two hands not only work separately, but also move too slowly and heavy-handedly (forgive the pun) to really make things work.

This results in a series of unhealthy and extreme ups and downs, known as a boom-bust cycle.

It used to be that you could buy a government-backed bond—one of the safest and most secure bonds out there—and get a return that would beat inflation. By keeping interest rates artificially low, the Federal Reserve has nearly eliminated the returns that taxpayers might ordinarily use to keep themselves afloat in inflationary times. Now, with this mess on our hands, the United States has broken its covenant with her people.

When a covenant is broken, it can have far-reaching consequences for the economy and financial markets. Inflation expectations may rise, leading to higher interest rates and reduced economic growth. Investors may lose confidence in the economy, leading to a flight from risky assets and a decline in asset prices. Ultimately, a broken covenant can lead to economic instability and uncertainty, which can have negative impacts on both individuals and businesses.

Despite the interference of Washington and Wall Street with small investors, there are still measures you can take to protect yourself.

Those things will be discussed in the coming chapters. For now, it's important to understand how we got here.

CHAPTER 2

HOW WE GOT HERE

"Those who do not remember the past are condemned to repeat it."

— George Santayana

We don't live in a vacuum—the past affects the present. Our current troubles began in the early 2000s.

In the late 90s President Bill Clinton balanced the budget, which was the last time we've had a balanced budget in this country. He took a combined approach, cutting government spending overall—including defense and welfare—and raising taxes on our top earners. We had budget surpluses for the fiscal years of 1998, 1999, 2000, and 2001, when he left office.[1]

From that point on, we were hit again and again with issues that shook our economy—and the world.

The attack on the World Trade Center in New York launched President George W. Bush's "War on Terror," sending troops to Afghanistan in 2001 and Iraq in 2003. Our defense budget grew to accommodate the needs of these wars and then some.

Then we were hit by the housing bubble of 2007 and the Great Recession of 2008, which caused federal spending to swell again.[2] People made less money, therefore paying less taxes and increasing the deficit.

To stimulate the economy, the Federal Reserve lowered interest rates to nearly zero and provided emergency loans—totaling $7.7 trillion—to failing banks. Several stimulus packages were passed to keep the worst at bay.[3]

When the dust settled in mid-2009, interest rates stayed historically low, remaining at nearly zero until 2015.[4] This manipulation of the interest rates may seem innocent, but it can (and did) have disastrous consequences.

If interest rates remain too low for an extended period of time, it creates an environment where too much money is chasing too few goods and services. The result? Rising prices.

After the financial crisis of 2008, central banks essentially flooded the economy with cheap money when they artificially kept interest rates down. However, since the supply of goods and services did not increase at the same pace, prices began to rise as businesses competed for a limited supply of goods and services. Over time, this increased demand for goods and services coupled with a limited supply has led to rising prices across a wide range of sectors—housing, food, and energy to name a few. This has eroded the purchasing power of our savings and incomes, ultimately contributing to the inflation we're experiencing today.

The Federal Reserve is responsible for these decisions. It has kept us out of trouble—and caused trouble—since its founding in 1913.

Before the founding of the Federal Reserve in 1913, we suffered through several financial panics and recessions. Bank panics—when people suddenly withdraw all their money from a bank in fear of the bank collapsing—were a relatively common phenomenon. The Panic of 1907 was particularly severe, with the stock market losing nearly 50% of its value and many banks and businesses failing.[5] High inflation was normal and had been since the founding of the country. These events were typically characterized by a rapid contraction of credit, widespread bank failures, and a sharp decline in economic activity.

Each of these financial panics and recessions had a significant impact on the U.S. economy and led to widespread suffering among ordinary Americans.

The lack of a central bank to provide liquidity and stabilize the financial system during these crises was seen as a major weakness of the United States economy. The Federal Reserve was established in response to this problem with the primary goal of promoting financial stability and economic growth. Regulating the money supply, setting interest rates, and providing a lender of last resort to banks in times of crisis are the main functions designed to achieve this goal.

The Federal Reserve helps keep our economy anchored

by alleviating or avoiding financial crises. To this day, the Federal Reserve acts as a watchdog against deteriorating economic structures, instituting monetary policies that protect our economy from falling apart.

However, it is quite remarkable that with each significant economic downturn the Federal Reserve's power and responsibilities have continued to expand. This has led to the creation of policies that are misguided and short-sighted, causing much of today's economic disruption rather than preventing it. Despite its creation to stabilize the economy and maintain the value of the dollar, the dollar's worth has plummeted by a staggering 98% since 1913.

Additionally, in times of war and economic strife, the government has repeatedly spent money it did not have. This has only further exacerbated the national debt crisis. It is concerning that despite these persistent issues little progress has been made to address them, and the trend of financial mismanagement continues.

Wars and recessions aren't the only contributors to our national debt. Recently Congress passed a $1.7 trillion bill that includes aid to Ukraine, climate change investments, financial assistance for students, childcare aid, military spending, and much more.[6]

I'm not going to express my personal opinion on the contents of this bill. But in light of mounting national debt and rising inflation, consider—should some of this money be spent differently?

It seems that a large part of the gaping national debt we face is due to a lack of responsibility from our government. If you were obligated to pay that $206,000 tomorrow, I bet you'd think more critically about legislation that builds in large-scale spending and how that spending is earmarked.

The absence of accountability is deeply concerning. It appears that our nation perpetually undermines its own progress without deriving valuable lessons from previous successes or failures.

With the government's irresponsible spending, ongoing international crises, rising inflation, and messy monetary policy, how will you safeguard your financial future?

What's your financial safety net when times (inevitably) get tougher? What's your plan for weathering economic storms?

I believe there are many viable solutions to address the problems I have identified. However, my preferred formula has been honed and polished over the years, and it is the solution I defer to when times get tough.

I'm happy to share it with you—in the next chapter.

CHAPTER 3

THINKING LIKE AN INVESTOR

"If everyone is thinking alike, then no one is thinking."

— Benjamin Franklin

How do you invest in a smart way, one that not only helps you grow your wealth but also shields you against the serious issues our economy faces today?

It's a question that looms large in the minds of many, especially in times of economic uncertainty. Our government's lack of responsibility has become a major contributing factor to the ever-growing national debt. As we grapple with these challenges, it's easy to feel frustrated or powerless, but it's crucial to remember that there are concrete steps we can take to protect ourselves and our financial future.

Everyone seems to have an opinion on how to invest wisely, so it's essential to sift through the noise and find a strategy that aligns with your goals and values.

Some might tell you to invest in the latest and most popular stocks—Meta (formerly known as Facebook),

Google, Apple, or Amazon. Others will advise that your best bet is in gold or silver.

Others will give you a spiel about "holistic investing," which is just as you would imagine it—making investment decisions that consider your complete financial picture.

Here's the crazy thing—nobody has the recipe for the secret sauce. There is no one-size-fits-all approach for investment success. Trends and fads come and go, but you can be a successful investor without following the latest fad just as much as you can be a successful investor without holding stock in Google or Apple.

How?

I'm a big fan of a combined approach—a dash of this, a splash of that—blending strategies and principles that have stood the test of time.

I call it *thinking like an investor*. Because the truth of the matter is that you don't have to be an economics major or an incredibly gifted mind to understand and thrive in the world of investing. All it takes is a little bit of common sense and more than two brain cells to rub together.

For me, there are seven investment principles that I live by that help me make smart decisions.

In the next few chapters, I'll delve into each of these principles and show you how each can take you far in your investing journey. I'll share stories and behind-the-scenes insights into some of the financial world's biggest blunders, triumphs, and scandals—you'll see from Blockbuster and Netflix to Bernie Madoff.

Before we do, though, here's a crash course on my seven investment principles.

1. **Stay in Your Comfort Zone.** Trust your instincts. If something smells off, it probably is. We'll discuss the importance of trusting your instincts in Chapters 4 and 5.

2. **Be Adaptable.** As mentioned, there is no secret sauce. If there was, it would tell you that successful investors change as the markets change. Stay with the times, if not a step ahead. Adaptability is key, and we'll cover it in Chapters 6 and 7.

3. **Think Critically.** Challenge the norm and dare to think differently—question the status quo. By doing so, you create space to find the undervalued gems that no one's investing in. Our discussions on critical thinking span across Chapters 4, 5, 6, and 7, and they comprise two essential facets.

    a. **Evaluating Your Financial Steward.** Take a closer look at the qualifications and intentions of the entity managing your finances. How can you ensure they have your best interests in mind? Are they genuinely aligned with your financial well-being?

b. **Analyzing Your Investment Choices.** Examine not just your investment choices, but also the rationale behind them. Is your choice truly a sound investment, or are there more suitable alternatives?

4. **Embrace Diversity.** Spread your net widely. Invest in an array of different businesses, industries, and even countries. We'll talk more about the benefits of diversification in Chapter 8.

5. **Have Patience.** Allow time and compound interest to let investments flourish. Patience is a virtue in investing, and we'll discuss it in Chapter 9.

6. **Get Creative.** Don't be afraid to break the mold—legally, of course. Invest in the future, not just in the past. We'll delve into creativity, especially how it relates to cryptocurrencies, in Chapter 11.

7. **Manage Risk.** Monitor your exposure to the inherently cyclical nature of the market—stay ahead of the wave rather than reacting to the tsunami. We'll handle risk management in Chapters 12 and 13.

These principles have shaped my investment approach, leading me to make well-informed and adventurous choices in an ever-evolving world of finance.

You might notice that many of these themes have overlapping touchpoints. Thinking critically and creativity have lots of similarities, for example. The same argument could be made for managing risk and staying diversified.

While I have tried my best to stick to one principle per chapter, the truth of the matter is that all of these principles essentially boil down to a fundamental question—as an investor, are you practical, rational, and levelheaded, or are you excitable, hasty, and reactive?

The former is the path that leads to success—I don't have to tell you where the latter goes.

Most of the above character traits (that you're either born with or you work on to develop) have similar underlying fundamentals, which is why you'll see a bit of overlap in the principles.

However, my hope is to bring the lofty world of investing down to Earth and talk about things you may not have considered, offering you insights into my process and perspective to help you preserve and grow your wealth.

We'll start in the center of the financial world—Wall Street.

CHAPTER 4

WALL STREET:

The Original Game of Thrones

"Wall Street is the only place that people ride to in a Rolls Royce to get advice from those who take the subway."

— Warren Buffett

In the realm of Wall Street—where financial powerhouses collide and fortunes are made and lost—the allure of all the potential gains can be extremely intoxicating.

You still have to be savvy, though—there are countless ways to invest and just as many ways to bankrupt yourself. The best way to avoid such a fate lies in your ability to think carefully and critically and exercise prudent judgment.

The realm of Wall Street is a double-edged sword fueled by an undercurrent of greed. Greed is a powerful, complex, and overwhelming emotion that can spur innovation and accomplishment—and it can also destroy lives, families, careers, and reputations.[1]

Wall Street is a battleground where power-hungry individuals are driven by the desire to amass wealth for themselves as part of building a grand financial empire.

Each of them engages in their personal battles with greed differently. Some win, some lose. The fallout can be bloody, grim, and shocking.

This is Game of Thrones in real life. The stories of individuals taking the wrong turn down Greed Street are countless, extending far beyond the confines of Wall Street itself. However, those within Wall Street possess the ability to access the wealth of others, and if they ignore their conscience you're in for a world of hurt.

Therefore, it is imperative for you to approach any Wall Street interaction with a sense of zealous self-protection.

I'll be the first to admit that it's a hard thing to do. In my business we want people to trust us. They have to if they're going to place their hard-earned money in our care. I also know people in the business who will say anything to get the deal done, even if it's not true. That's not how I roll, but I've seen enough to know that you have to be careful. I cannot state this strongly enough—you have to be careful.

It doesn't help that psychologically we're practically wired to trust people automatically—even strangers.

Tim Levine, a psychologist from the University of Alabama, calls it the truth-default theory.[2] The theory posits that in human communication we tend to believe others implicitly, and it doesn't occur to us that perhaps we should double-check. Levine notes that our automatic assumptions of truth are good because it's necessary for "communication to function" and because "most people are mostly honest most of the time."

However, the truth-default mechanism makes it easy to pull the wool over our eyes. "On average," Levine writes, "judges correctly identify liars 54% of the time—just slightly better than chance. This is true no matter who does the judging. Students are terrible. FBI agents are terrible. CIA officers are terrible. Lawyers are terrible. There may be people who beat the odds. But if there are, they are rare."[3] We only detect liars when the lie is so outlandish we're forced to conclude that it is a lie.

In a world where the little guy's interests are rarely prioritized, it's crucial to look out for yourself—even if you're not such a little guy. *Especially* if you're not a little guy. (The more money you have, the more you can lose. If you're wealthy, you're a big fish for the wrong kinds of people.)

So, how do you beat the odds? What are the warning signs that something is amiss? How do you navigate the treacherous waters of investing while safeguarding against potential harm? These are questions that demand careful consideration.

Earlier I mentioned that it's crucial to stay in your comfort zone while investing. This applies in many different ways. Namely, if something or someone smells fishy to you and you can't shake that feeling, trust it. Go with your gut. I've never seen someone take a cautious approach to investing and feel sorry about it.

There's an old saying that I often find myself repeating—there are plenty of people in the country club who sold too early, but none who sold too late.

Those who throw caution to the wind are taking on unnecessary and excessive risks that could very easily lead to their downfall. Making calculated, well-thought-out risks and pulling back when appropriate is an act of preserving wealth, not being a wimp.

As we've discussed, there are a lot of things that require careful consideration before venturing into the realm of investing.

Let's start with the individuals entrusted with guiding and managing your financial interests. What should you be wary of? What should you be looking out for? How do you spot a swindler? What are the red flags and telltale signs to watch out for?

To answer this, we'll delve into the captivating tale of the most notorious figure on Wall Street—Bernie Madoff.

CHAPTER 5

THE RISE AND FALL OF BERNIE MADOFF:

A Cautionary Tale of Unchecked Power and Fraud

"There are three things in the world that deserve no mercy, hypocrisy, fraud, and tyranny."

— Frederick William Robertson

In September of 2008, I threw a fit at an important board meeting for a local organization.

Believe it or not, it was one of my better moments.

A fellow board member suggested using some funds to invest with Bernie Madoff, increasing our bottom line. They reasoned that Bernie was always up—we couldn't possibly lose. Several others agreed, but I vehemently did not. I told my colleagues that if they decided to invest with Madoff I'd quit and wouldn't return.

When it came to Madoff, I could tell something was off.

It was more than just a nagging feeling, though. Although Madoff's operations were largely unknown to the public, those within the industry knew of his dealings for several years. My business partner, Peter, was a floor trader and eventually the Governor of the New York Stock Exchange (NYSE) at the time. With his help, we poked around about Madoff. We always got the same answer—although Madoff was managing billions of dollars, no one had ever seen a trade from his shop. Peter himself had never seen a trade, even as Governor.

It seemed highly unlikely that he was managing that amount of money—completely in compliance with the law—without a single person on the NYSE trading floor witnessing a transaction from him.

That was all the information I needed. I had no way of knowing what Madoff was up to, but I knew that he was bad news.

It turns out I was right.

On December 11, 2008, Bernie Madoff was arrested for running the biggest Ponzi scheme in history, estimated at $64.8 billion in losses. His victims—including high-profile names like Steven Spielberg and Kevin Bacon—lost life savings and inheritances, rattling the financial world forever.[1]

His entire hedge fund was a hoax—millions of transactions over nearly 30 years were completely falsified. It was stunning in its complete duplicity.[2]

The infamous scam starts (kind of) with a man named Charles Ponzi.[3]

In 1919, Italian immigrant Charles Ponzi founded a company that allowed people to pre-purchase postage to include in their letters—known as international reply coupons (IRCs). These coupons could be taken to a post office and exchanged for local postage stamps to reply to the original letter.[4] For example, an IRC could be purchased in Spain for 30 centavos, sent in a letter to the United States, and then "exchanged for a US postage stamp worth 5 cents, a redemption rate that was fixed by international treaty."[5]

IRCs were groundbreaking at the time. Previously, international mail had been finicky due to constantly changing exchange rates, making postage an expensive endeavor that one could easily waste money on. Ponzi made IRCs easy to access and business boomed. The company was legitimate and people wanted the opportunity to invest.

Ponzi went on and founded the Securities Exchange Company, allowing people to invest in his postage business and raise capital to buy more postage abroad. It was a win-win situation—he guaranteed a 50% return within 45 days of investing and a 100% return within 90 days.

His success with the international reply coupons attracted thousands of investors, but rather than invest the money he pulled off what is now known as a Ponzi scheme. The scheme operated by paying old investors with cash from new investors, fulfilling his promise of 100% return within 90 days.

During the first eight months of 1920, Ponzi earned $15 million from his scam (around $230 million in today's dollars).[6]

He told investors he could guarantee such an incredible return because he capitalized on "fluctuating currency values," allowing him to purchase stamps at a lower rate abroad and sell them for face value in the United States.[7] This is known as the legal practice of arbitrage—buying a security in one market and selling it at a higher price in a different one, benefiting from the difference.[8]

Because of the exchange rates in other countries, for example, "someone who bought a postal reply coupon in Spain could redeem it in the United States for about a 10% profit. Purchasing coupons in countries with weaker economies could increase that margin substantially."[9] Ponzi had been utilizing arbitrage to build his lucrative IRC business throughout his short tenure in the industry before his scheme began. However, arbitrage generally does not produce the significant return on investment that Ponzi was promising—or delivering.

Instead, he was simply recycling money through old and new investors to keep his promises. Unlike arbitrage, this is not a legal practice.

The scam continued even after the Universal Postal Union caught on to his arbitrage business and stopped selling international reply coupons. To get around this bump in the road, Ponzi told investors he'd cultivated a sophisticated group of agents buying postage for him worldwide. This was a lie.

People were so stunned by the money he was making them that they didn't question it. When they did, he declined to tell them the more intimate details of his transactions.

Ponzi was a very popular figure at the time and the newspapers raved about him.

> *"Whoever said that proud old New Englanders are conservative undoubtedly made that statement before the advent of Charles Ponzi. Today all of Boston is get-rich-quick mad over him, the creator of fortunes, the modern King Midas who doubles your money in ninety days. Did I say Boston? My mistake. I should have said the entire New England, from Calais, Maine to Lake Champlain, from the Canadian border to New Jersey.*
>
> *"At every corner, on the street-cars, behind the department store counters, from luxurious parlors to humble kitchens, to the very outskirts of New England, Ponzi is making more hope, more anxiety, than any conquering general of old. Mary Pickford, Sir Thomas Lipton, and smuggling booze over the Canadian border aren't in it anymore.*
>
> *"For Ponzi makes everybody rich quick. Loan him your money, from fifty dollars to fifty thousand dollars, and in*

180 days, he gives you back twice as much as you gave him. He has been doing it for eight months and is still at it.

"With no other security than his personal note, Boston is pouring all its savings into Ponzi's hands. Like a tidal wave, the passion for investment with the new Italian banker has swept over Boston folk until it took half of Boston's police force to subdue the enthusiasm of a throng of prospective investors overflowing from the banking office, through the corridors, down the stairs, and into the street, blocking the traffic."[10]

He was caught in the latter half of 1920, and the notoriety forever attached his name to the scam.

Charles Ponzi was not the first person to execute such a scheme, but his fraud was the largest of his time. Ponzi schemes have been traced to the late 1800s, often called "Rob Peter to pay Paul" schemes because the perpetrators pay off early investors with money from later investors.[11]

Bernie Madoff's Ponzi scheme was similar to Ponzi's in that he promised investors high returns with little risk. However, Madoff's scheme was much larger and more complex. Madoff was arrested in 2008 and sentenced to 150 years in prison. He died in prison in 2021.

Since Charles Ponzi, hundreds of thousands of similar schemes have materialized in nearly every country and industry with devastating results.[12] As technology has become more sophisticated, so have Ponzi schemes. While Ponzi's scam lasted less than a year, Bernie Madoff's was much more intricate, technologically advanced, and difficult to trace. This allowed him to continue for decades unnoticed.

Old dogs don't learn new tricks, but ostensibly they know the old ones. For such an old trick, Ponzi schemes often go undetected until it's too late. For that reason, Ponzi schemes are still a relatively popular phenomenon.

As an example, in October 2021 an actor named Zachary Horowitz was sentenced to 20 years in prison for running a $650 million Ponzi scheme in Hollywood.[13] He convinced investors that he could license foreign films to major streamers like HBO and Netflix with returns of more than 25%. In reality, these films didn't exist—and neither did the licenses.

But let's go back to Bernie. While there are still many murky details surrounding him and his scam, we do know some pretty key points about the life and times of Mr. Madoff.

Born in 1938 in Queens, New York, Madoff was a familiar face on Wall Street. After graduating from Hofstra University in 1960, he worked as a lifeguard and installed sprinkler systems.[14] He began to trade penny stocks—shares of a small company worth less than $5—with the money he'd earned from those ventures.[15]

In 1960, he founded Bernard L. Madoff Investment Securities and gained a reputation as a savvy investor and market maker—the practice of matching sellers of stock with buyers and brokering the deal. However, his success was overshadowed by the feeling that he didn't belong to the "it crowd" on Wall Street.[16]

The exclusion from the "it crowd" on Wall Street fueled Madoff's determination, leading him to adopt a more aggressive approach and engage in transactions that larger and more reputable firms would dismiss.

He kept at it, and his experience with penny stocks gave him the expertise to help form the Nasdaq stock exchange, modernizing the industry. By the late 80s, Madoff's company was responsible for a whopping 9% of all New York Stock Exchange transactions.[17] He served as the chairman of the Nasdaq for three one-year terms in 1990, 1991, and 1993.[18]

It's unclear when Madoff took a wrong turn down the darkest alley of Greed Street and never looked back. It seems to have started around the same time he founded his market-making business in the early 60s.[19] Alongside his market-making, Madoff had a side hustle—investment advisory. He started small with family members and friends, but his returns were so impressive that word spread—more people wanted in.

Two accountants in his father-in-law's company—Michael Bienes and Frank Avellino—began collecting investors and funneling money to Madoff for him to invest. Other “feeder funds” appeared over time, including private banks, financiers, aristocrats, royal families, and the Hollywood elite. His clientele stretched across continents and generations.[20]

The nature of the feeder funds gave him a certain amount of detachment and anonymity, which he preferred. The SEC went after Bienes and Avellino for acting as unlicensed investment advisors, but the investigation never reached Madoff’s doorstep. The feeder funds kept the SEC off his trail.[21]

His business was essentially split into two—his legitimate, well-known market-making company that employed his two sons and brother, and his under-the-radar hedge fund that housed the Ponzi scheme. The double business existed under the same name and was located in the same office building, just floors away from each other.[22]

When people asked questions about their investments, they were brushed off or intimidated out of asking anything else. Often, investors got a nice, consistent return on investment, making it hard to ask questions. The most anyone got out of Madoff about his investment philosophy was that he used a split-strike conversion strategy.

Feeder fund managers didn’t raise any questions either. They seemed content to turn a blind eye and were incentivized not to inquire further, as revealed in a Senate hearing in 2009. The Fairfield Greenwich group—one of Madoff's largest feeder funds with about $7.2 billion invested with him—was founded by sophisticated, seasoned professionals in the industry.[23] Their complete disregard of the warning signs, despite their industry experience, remains an appalling fact.

People were so caught up in Madoff's success that *The New York Times* reported that by 1992, "hedge funds, pension plans, and university endowments were entrusting hundreds of millions of dollars to Mr. Madoff—despite a business operation that was cloaked in secrecy, account statements that were suspiciously antiquated, and independent audits that a one-man firm signed in a suburban storefront office."[24]

These weren't the only red flags fluttering in the breeze.

Unbeknownst to Madoff, a group of risk analysts in Boston were curious about his consistent returns and began to investigate. Frank Casey and Harry Markopolos—investors at Rampart Investment Management in Boston—spent about four hours using publicly available information to reverse-engineer Madoff's investment strategy. They had been hoping to use his strategy to get the same returns, if it was legitimate.[25]

What they discovered was that there was no investment strategy. It was a Ponzi scheme.

Harry Markopolos called on the SEC to investigate in 2000.

Markopolos also notified an investigative journalist, and several publications picked up the story in 2001. Just the fact that Madoff managed billions of dollars in investments when he was well-known as a market-maker was worthy of the front page. The SEC investigation, however, could not find anything amiss with Madoff and *let him off the hook.*

Markopolos wasn't the only person who had major doubts about Bernie Madoff. His status as an outsider on Wall Street remained to a certain degree, and people wondered if he was engaging in insider trading or front running to achieve his returns.

At the time, industry insiders didn't know what Madoff was up to—they just knew they didn't want to touch him with a ten-foot pole. Markopolos noted in the third of his five complaints between 2000 and 2005 to the SEC that "Madoff is suspected of being a fraud by some of the world's largest and most sophisticated financial service firms."[26]

If it was something Wall Street insiders knew, why didn't they turn him into the SEC? As Markopolos says, very succinctly, "people in glass houses don't throw stones, and self-regulation on Wall Street doesn't work."[27] In other words, no one wants the SEC breathing down their neck, so they'd rather keep their mouths shut than accidentally open an investigation on their firms. Plus, no one really had any idea what was going on—they just knew something wasn't right. A bad feeling isn't enough to point accusatory fingers.

It seems crazy that the SEC brushed off something so obvious that took Markopolos only four hours to figure out and was somewhat common knowledge on Wall Street. However, Madoff had a few things going for him.

First and foremost, the SEC was severely understaffed and could not complete an investigation with the diligence a Ponzi scheme like Madoff's required.

Years later, an investigation into the SEC's Madoff failures found that "the SEC received more than ample information in the form of detailed and substantive complaints over the years to warrant a thorough and comprehensive examination or investigation of Bernard Madoff...for operating a Ponzi scheme, and that despite three examinations and two investigations being conducted, a thorough and competent investigation or examination was never performed."[28]

In 2005, Markopolos submitted his second explicitly detailed complaint to the SEC which identified almost 30 red flags that pointed to Madoff's fraud. In his opening remarks, he noted, "I [am] very suspicious that Bernie Madoff's returns aren't real. [I]f they are real, then they would almost certainly have to be generated by front-running customer order flow from the broker-dealer arm of Madoff Investment Securities, LLC."[29]

In all investigations of Madoff—from 1992 (with Bienes and Avellino) until he confessed in 2008—the SEC was sloppy, careless, and took Madoff's word at face value. All this despite grave allegations.

Second, Madoff's scam was technologically sophisticated in a rather unconventional way. After modernizing the industry with Nasdaq, Madoff had a taste for cutting-edge technology. His brokerage firm utilized top-of-the-line computers and software, and the hedge fund was similarly cloaked in tech.

Using a popular IBM database management system called AS/400, Madoff had programmers use an older form of coding—RPG II—to create fake transcripts of trades automatically. Where Charles Ponzi had to juggle his fraud manually, Bernie Madoff let the computers do the grunt work.

Longtime RPG coder Rich Diedrich was tasked with unraveling Madoff's code when the scheme imploded. It took him a long time to untangle all of it—he had to build tools to help him run and understand code totaling 20,000 HTML pages. The complexity of the code helped Madoff throw off the SEC and suspicious investors.

"For the audit, they needed to have counter-trade trades. You needed to have who you were buying from, who you were selling from, the blocks you were buying and selling," he explains. "They had to essentially create all the documentation for the trades. So they had a program that would go out and essentially take a trade and then split it into sub-trades, and then it would go through and generate all the reports of all the trading tickets. They could print them all out."[30]

Madoff was a confident and reassuring face to many investors. Though many came to him through feeder funds (and did not know he was managing their money), many knew and interacted with him. Ponzi schemes require the influx of new money to keep everything from falling apart, but Madoff was a master manipulator—he threw people a curveball they never saw coming.

Instead of playing desperate, Madoff famously made it seem impossible to invest with him. Exclusivity was—and still is—extremely appealing in a world of VIP sections and private schools. You had to know someone to get into his fund, as he was firmly closed to new investors.

He played the cautious investor, too. One associate told the Wall Street Journal that, with new clients, he would encourage them to take things slowly. "Bernie would tell me, 'Let them start small, and if they're happy the first year or two, they can put in more.'"[31]

His real money, he told people, was in his market-making business. His side hustle appeared to be a favor he did for friends and family. As The New Yorker put it, he "posed as a man beleaguered by his own generosity, who took on new clients as a favor to friends."[32]

In this respect, he was telling the truth. He didn't need

investors or a Ponzi scheme to make money. His legal, above-board brokerage firm was bringing him just north of $100 million a year by the late 80s.[33] He admitted to New York Magazine journalist Steve Fishman that he didn't know why he'd scammed so many people. He shared, "I had more than enough money to support my lifestyle and my family's lifestyle. I didn't need to do this for that."[34]

To complete the picture of a confident, seasoned investor, Madoff was well-spoken and poised. "In today's regulatory environment," he said at a speaking engagement in 2007, "it's virtually impossible to violate rules…certainly not for a considerable period of time."[35]

Wise words from the king of all con men.

As the 2008 financial crash waged war on the market, investors began clamoring to Madoff to loosen up some extra change. Losing control of the scam, Madoff saw the beginning of the end as money bled out. On the evening of December 10, 2008, he confessed to his sons, brother, and wife that it was all "one big lie" and he was billions of dollars in debt. His sons alerted the SEC and Madoff was arrested the next day.

At that point, though, it was too late. Madoff had gotten away with swindling nearly 5,000 accounts—an estimated 11,000 individuals and countless banks, charities, investment firms, insurance companies, synagogues, universities, and hedge funds.[36] The scam stretched from

New York to South Korea, France, the United Kingdom, Switzerland, Spain, Japan, Israel, Austria, and Germany.

Madoff's accomplices included his RPG programmers George Perez and Jerome O'Hara, chief financial officer Frank DiPascali, brother Peter Madoff, and investor Jeffry Picower (among others). All have faced massive repercussions for their part in the scam.

Madoff's son Mark and feeder fund manager Rene-Thierry Magon de la Villehuchet were so plagued by guilt that they took their own lives in the years following Madoff's arrest.[37] After losing their life savings, at least two of Madoff's victims died by suicide.

The SEC suffered a nightmarish blow to its reputation. The Madoff scandal is widely considered to be the SEC's biggest failure. In the post-Madoff era, the SEC made comprehensive changes to their structure, from changing how it handles tips to hiring new leadership.[38]

The biggest fallout, however, was how investment behavior changed in the wake of Bernie Madoff. According to a study from Cornell, "Investors yanked $363 billion from the financial advisers they had entrusted with it—even though many of those advisers had nothing to do with Madoff—and stashed a significant portion into safe assets such as bank deposits."[39]

As we've discussed, money gets moldy in bank accounts—especially with high inflation like we saw in

2008. So what can we learn from Madoff?

First, know that several key markers can indicate that someone is running a Ponzi scheme:

- Promising high, virtually zero-risk return on investment
- Providing consistent returns regardless of market conditions
- Operating without registration with the Securities and Exchange Commission (SEC) as an investment company
- Exhibiting cagey and secretive behavior when it comes to disclosing investment strategies
- Enjoying high visibility which may lead to a false sense of credibility
- Putting pressure on individuals to invest hastily and sometimes restricting investment opportunities to an "exclusive" group, creating an aura of inaccessibility that enhances their appeal.[40]

Additionally, SEC regulations require that all private funds:

- Conduct annual external audits
- Have third-party administrators (accountants) who set the net asset value independently

- Hold all customer funds at well-established banking institutions that provide another layer of security.

If you want to invest with a specific individual, check that the major players are registered and licensed properly before giving them any dollars. Once you've invested, watch your statements for overwhelming consistency or signs that things aren't adding up.

Take everything with a grain of salt; do not mindlessly trust the people you're asking to handle your money. In the courts, you're innocent until proven guilty. On Wall Street, it's the opposite—you're a liar until proven trustworthy. Much of Madoff's scam existed before the Internet, but now you have much more information at your fingertips. Doing your due diligence isn't just safe or essential, it's easy. There was no excuse to ignore it back then, and even more so now.

Madoff preyed on his community—synagogues, Jewish charities, and his friends and family were not spared from his greed. Famous Holocaust survivor Elie Wiesel lost all of his life savings and $15 million from his foundation—the Elie Wiesel Foundation for Humanity—to Madoff. [41]

Bottom line—just because someone is part of your community doesn't mean you can blindly give them your trust. People from your neighborhood, church, or local gym need as much verification as a stranger.

Investing is a fusion of art and science, but simplicity

is at its core. If alarm bells ring because you cannot grasp how your money is being invested and no one can explain clearly, pay attention. You should consider taking your money elsewhere.

Moreover, if you feel discouraged or threatened from asking questions—any question at all—take your money and run. It's your money, so you're better off asking the questions and not liking the answers than losing a good chunk of your portfolio to a scammer.

There are other questions you should be asking when it comes to investing, aside from assessing whether or not the business is a scam. Examining your investments' viability and ability to produce a return is the other side of the coin of critical thinking. We'll discuss how thinking critically could have saved Blockbuster in the next chapter.

CHAPTER 6

BLOCKBUSTER BREAKTHROUGHS:

Harnessing Critical Thinking and Adaptability for Success

"All happy companies are different: each one earns a monopoly by solving a unique problem. All failed companies are the same: they failed to escape competition."

— Peter Thiel

I'm sure one day I'll mention Blockbuster to my future grandchildren and they'll look at me blankly.

The rotary phone, milkmen, cable TV—heck, even maskless entry to the hospital—are things of the past.

It's nature—things are born and things die. But sometimes death comes earlier than expected and seems so avoidable—you can't help but wonder what went wrong?

That's what I think about when Blockbuster comes to mind.

Founded by David Cook in 1985, Blockbuster was a smashing success. Blockbuster was different from other video rental stores because of its innovation. It provided customers with a massive selection of tapes—nearly 8,000—while competitors could only manage hundreds.[1] Cook was a software engineer and his stores offered a huge selection thanks to a new barcode system that allowed them to keep track of thousands of titles.

A year into the business, Cook was able to expand to four stores. By 1986, the company was sold to a trio of investors—Wayne Huizenga, John Melk, and Scott Beck—for $18.5 million. Cook left the company in 1987 and Huizenga took the helm. At that time, Blockbuster had 20 locations and continued growing aggressively under Huizenga's direction. They began buying out other video rental chains and opening new stores.[2]

Less than ten years later, Blockbuster opened its 1,000th store.[3] By then there were locations in Canada, Mexico, the United Kingdom, Ireland, and Australia.[4] Huizenga sold Blockbuster to Viacom in 1994 for $8.4 billion, and the sale was the beginning of the end—Blockbuster began to circle the drain.

When Blockbuster was founded, video rental was the only way for people to watch movies after they left the theaters. People headed to a Blockbuster branch in their area to rent and rewatch an old favorite or catch the latest films. Blockbuster was the undisputed king of the movie industry.

Under Viacom, Blockbuster began to expand its focus.

Music and video games were available to rent, as well as MTV merchandise, toys, books, and clothing.[5] This was the first of a series of fumbles under Viacom's management—by 1996 Blockbuster had lost half of its market value.

A large part of Blockbuster's success was its payment model—people paid to rent movies, and Blockbuster also charged a $40 fee for tapes that were not returned on time. The late fees made Blockbuster $800 million in its heyday, which was about 16% of its revenue.[6] People hated the late fees, none more than Silicon Valley software engineer Reed Hastings.

The story goes that Hastings founded Netflix in 1997 after incurring the detestable $40 fee for returning "Apollo 13" late.[7] Although Netflix is now a major movie streamer and producer, it began as a DVD rental company. People could have movies sent directly to their homes for a flat monthly fee. The best part was they didn't charge late fees. Ever.

Hastings said in an interview:

"I remember the fee because I was embarrassed about it. That was back in the VHS days, and it got me thinking that there's a big market out there.

So I started to investigate the idea of how to create a movie-rental business by mail. I didn't know about DVDs, and then a friend of mine told me they were coming.

I ran out to Tower Records in Santa Cruz, California, and mailed CDs to myself, just a disc in an envelope. It was a long 24 hours until the mail arrived back at my house, and I ripped them open, and they were all in great shape. That was the big excitement point."[8]

Netflix was small but steadily gaining speed until the dot-com bubble of the early 2000s, which put immense pressure on the small company. Hastings offered Blockbuster CEO John Antioco a chance to buy Netflix for $50 million, telling him, "We will run the online part of the combined business; you'll focus on the stores. We'll find the synergies that come from the combination, and it will truly be a case of the whole being greater than the sum of its parts."[9]

But Antioco passed, thinking it was a joke. He wrote that he "firmly believed we could keep the Blockbuster brand relevant, no matter how people decided to watch movies."[10]

Hastings was humbled. He admitted on a podcast in 2020 that after the fateful Blockbuster meeting, "I had this image of all sixty thousand Blockbuster employees erupting in laughter at the ridiculousness of our proposal…Why would a powerhouse like Blockbuster, with millions of customers, massive revenues, a talented CEO, and a brand synonymous with home movies, be interested in a flailing wannabe like Netflix? What could we possibly offer that they couldn't do more effectively themselves?"[11]

Many might have given up at that point—facing losses of about $57 million—but Hastings kept at it.

By 2004, another competitor—Redbox—entered the scene. Blockbuster still outstripped Netflix and Redbox, with 9,000 stores worldwide making $5.9 billion in revenue. But Netflix and Redbox were innovating, and Blockbuster was stagnating. Blockbuster parted ways with Viacom and John Antioco around this time.

In 2007, Netflix had 6.3 million subscribers and started revolutionizing the movie-watching business like Blockbuster had done when it began. They now offered streaming, a new way to watch. Instead of a physical VHS tape or DVD, you could download the movie directly to your TV or computer and watch from there. No need to hassle with pickups or returns—just click and watch.

Blockbuster had toyed with video-on-demand in a partnership with Enron, ultimately bringing Blockbuster Online to life in the early 2000s.[12] But Antioco felt so strongly about the potential of the brick-and-mortar establishments that they walked away from Enron and Blockbuster Online by the end of 2001. It had cost them $200 million to create. Blockbuster also decided to eliminate late fees, which had become the Achilles heel of their business. They were overly dependent on the late fees, but in the name of keeping Blockbuster alive they took the plunge—this cost them another $200 million.[13]

In the years following Viacom's departure, Blockbuster lost 75% of its market value.[14] Netflix grew and grew, nibbling away at Blockbuster until 2010 when Blockbuster declared bankruptcy.

There are many reasons why Netflix pulled ahead of Blockbuster in the end. One was a slimmer business model. Compared to Blockbuster, Netflix didn't have much overhead. They didn't have to rent, buy, or maintain retail space, they could offer a greater variety of movies to customers as they had more space—both digitally and physically—and they utilized a subscription service that made late fees obsolete while bringing in money monthly.

But the main reason for Netflix's victory was that Blockbuster was too set on the old model and didn't recognize the market had changed. They missed crucial chances to get ahead—or catch up—and couldn't see a future where brick-and-mortar stores or physical movie copies would be antiquated.

This is where thinking critically might have saved them. Hindsight is 20/20, but as VHS tapes morphed into DVDs, it wasn't hard to imagine a future where you might not need a physical copy to play a movie.

Blockbuster was a victim of their own prosperity. They were so successful in the video rental space that they didn't see the need to change. They were too late when they realized that change was necessary. Unfortunately, it cost them a late fee of far more than $40.

As an investor, you need to critically examine everything. Can the company I'm investing in weather changes in technology and the market? Can they stay relevant for the next 25 (or more) years?

I learned this lesson very clearly in 1993. My wife worked for a Canadian cable company that Comcast had recently purchased. At a work event, my wife and I met Comcast CEO Brian Roberts. We had a pleasant discussion, but I wanted to pick his brain about something.

"What's your biggest fear?" I asked.

"Satellite," he answered almost immediately.

At the time I knew nothing about satellites, so I did some research after the event.

I discovered that Dish Network and DirectTV were just getting started, and Dish was doing a bond offering to raise capital to get a satellite up. After some thought, I realized that their only cost would be marketing once they got that satellite up. I took the chance and invested.

Throughout the rest of the 90s, their stock prices remained low—never hitting more than $6 a share. But in the early 2000s, it jumped up to almost $75.[15] They had a few downswings and upswings, but my bet was solid—I made about 40 times my money. My wife was shocked.

I was more impressed with Brian Roberts, though. He had his eye on the future—he knew what was coming and was thinking about it. He knew he had to figure out how to pivot Comcast in the next five years to survive the changes in technology and market demand.

He recognized that his business couldn't stay relevant forever and wasn't afraid of the change. Instead of avoiding change, he embraced it. Since then, they have continued to innovate to keep themselves afloat.

As an investor, it's imperative to recognize the ever-shifting tides and emerging trends in the market and be willing to adapt to them accordingly. Adaptability is a unique skill all investors must possess.

Things change constantly. This is true for all industries over time. Progress pushes us forward, unseating the past. We must move with the tide to avoid being swept up in it.

In less than a hundred years we've gone from horse and buggy to cars. General stores have morphed into Amazon warehouses. Humphry Davie's Electric Arc lamps have become LED light bulbs.[16] Streaming has dominated the TV and movie industry, as well as the music industry. Thomas Edison's phonographs became vinyl LPs, cassette tapes, and then CDs. Now all of us have Spotify or Apple Music playing the songs we love, directly into Bluetooth headphones. Popular culture has shaped the course of innovation, too. Apple iPhone and Samsung Galaxy phones are the cutting edge of innovation thanks to their ancestors, Blackberry and Palm.

It takes time to see how the tides will turn and which

industries or innovations have more potential than others, but things are always changing. We're constantly moving, just as the Earth is always revolving around the sun—ignoring this fact is a dangerous way to do things. However, so is completely rebranding or changing course every five years. Notice that Brian Roberts didn't pivot into a satellite TV company—he just watched and waited, knowing that things would change and he would need to be prepared for those changes.

Reed Hastings is another example of this, just on the other side of the coin. He knew he was pushing the industry toward the future with DVDs and video on demand, but it took a few years to get there. He kept moving forward by taking calculated, thought-out risks. As of September 2023, Netflix has a market cap of $196.22 billion. This makes Netflix the world's 54th most valuable company by market cap.[17]

The question is, do you have stock in the next Netflix or are you putting your hard-earned money into something that will just crash and burn?

Ultimately, it goes back to critical thinking. Can you take yourself out of the equation? Can you imagine where the needle is pointing in innovation? Can you dismantle any assumptions you might have about the company or market? Can you change things when you figure out that you're heading in the wrong direction?

In more practical terms, here are some things I suggest you think about when considering an investment.

1. **What is the size of the market?** Is there a need or demand that will continually or regularly generate new business?

2. **Consider a 30,000-foot view.** Overall, what do the trends in the macro market—or majority of consumers—indicate about the status of the investment's past, present, and future?

3. **Is the company well-capitalized?** Get your hands on the financials and assess whether the company can easily access cash to cover its obligations, both short-term and long-term. Additionally, can it handle unexpected downturns, regulations, or use excess capital to innovate appropriately?

4. **Does the leadership have a vision for the future?** Do they have the capacity and ability to execute their vision? Is it a vision you agree with or feel is important for the general market?

A great example of a company that displayed these traits is the Palm cell phone company. Starting with the Palm Pilot personal digital assistant (PDA) in 1996, this innovative, useful, and affordable technology was a massive hit.[18] They continued revolutionizing hand-held tech, ushering in the age of the smartphone. In 2000, Palm was worth more than Apple, Amazon, and Google *combined.*

Google (Alphabet) is another excellent example. Contrary to popular belief, they were not the first search engine—not by a long shot.[19] However, they were the best because they provided (and still provide) the most accurate results that were supported by complex algorithms that made the user's experience seamless and simple.

How do you find a company like Google or Palm before they get big?

A lot of that answer has to do with keeping your eye on the market, thinking outside the box, and patiently waiting for the right moment.

We'll talk about thinking outside the box—challenging the status quo—in the next chapter.

CHAPTER 7

FUELING THE FUTURE:

Navigating Fossil Fuel Dependence and Climate Change as an Investor

"You can resist an invading army. You cannot resist an idea whose time has come."

— Victor Hugo

At the beginning of this book, we discussed how Washington tends to pollute the economic climate rather than preserve it. When it comes to the actual climate, there are more than enough preservation efforts going on.

I have two issues with this. First, the costs of most renewable energy sources are prohibitive and less efficient than traditional energy sources, making them a chronically poor decision from an economical standpoint. Second, aggressively forcing environmental change through legislation adds to the massive national debt (which seems to be less and less of an issue these days).

I'm not trying to imply that climate change is a hoax or that the issues are mutually exclusive. We must focus on climate change, just as we must focus on the national debt and other economic issues. As a lover of nature and the great outdoors (especially in Florida!), I'm increasingly concerned about climate change. But sometimes I wonder how realistic we're being.

General consensus is that the heavy use of fossil fuels around the world is causing our planet to warm, slowly destroying ecosystems, polluting the air, and messing with the Earth's finely-tuned balance. Some estimates say we'll see the disastrous consequences of our dependence come to a head as soon as the next decade, and some posit that it's still a little while away.

Either way, it's an issue that demands attention to mitigate as much damage as possible—for us, our children, and the generations ahead.

It's hard to know what's coming. Unfortunately, we're not prophets, so timing the end of the world is little more than a guess. It's easy to invalidate, rationalize, or make light of the issue. It's also easy to become paranoid, scared, or militant.

You only know the past and present—the future is out of our grasp. There's a lot of denial and fear-mongering out there, so staying in the rational middle lane on issues like these—especially because it affects all of us deeply—is not easy. I don't blame anyone who takes either side on the issue. The matter of our planet is foundational to everything else, and it can be both tough to face and tough to ignore.

On the other hand, an inordinate amount of time and

money is put into regulation and legislation that sometimes seems counterintuitive when considering the behemoth economic issues we face. This is especially true since there is a tremendous amount that we don't understand about our world and climate. What's true? What's false? It's never really clear. Therefore, it can be extraordinarily frustrating in difficult economic times to hear a sermon on the importance of green, clean—ridiculously expensive—energy.

We're finding that greener, cleaner solutions are just as polluting as fossil fuels and significantly less efficient. To make matters worse, it's become a terribly partisan issue, making it nearly impossible to compromise on the subject.

"Clean" products that exist today—like electric cars—are far from perfect. Elon Musk's Tesla Motors is an impressive feat of technological finesse. But just like our cell phones, laptops, and many other electronic products, electric cars rely on elements like lithium, cobalt, and nickel in their batteries.

These trace elements are not renewable, are scarce, and require mining deep into the earth—using machines powered by fossil fuels, no less—to access and use them in batteries.[1]

Furthermore, lithium-ion batteries have a lifespan—once that is over, they sit in landfills and leak toxic chemicals into the ground.[2] That is, if they don't cause massive fires first.[3] At the end of their life, these batteries become particularly susceptible to combustion—especially if they end up in garbage trucks or waste facilities. Lithium-ion batteries should be recycled, but it is a delicate and intricate process, and most people don't realize they have to.[4]

Other green options aren't so great either. Nuclear energy is stymied by regulation and misunderstanding, as well as serious safety concerns.[5] Solar panels don't work in overcast areas and take up vast swaths of space, as well as being particularly vulnerable to cyber attacks.[6] Wind turbines kill countless bats and birds, and harnessing the power of the water and waves is impeded by saltwater and barnacles.[7] Many of these renewable energy sources depend on fossil fuels to build anyway, and they have a shorter lifespan than fossil fuels.

A prime example is solar panels. A generally good idea for renewable energy, they have about a 30-year lifespan. A recent study found that "8 million metric tons of these panels will have reached the end of their working lives by 2030, a tally that is projected to reach 80 million [metric tons] by 2050."[8]

Recycling these panels presents a huge problem. The technology is inefficient, expensive, and underused, so old panels are left to decay in landfills where they—like lithium-ion batteries—leak toxic chemicals and cause more pollution.

Even in Europe—where recycling old solar panels is

required by law—many plants simply recycle the aluminum and glass parts of the panels, and the rest is reduced to ashes, burning up trace elements like silver, copper, and silicon.[9]

Plus, because these solar panels were made to withstand weather of all kinds, even taking them apart is a major undertaking.

The more panels we use over time, the more waste happens—polluting the environment the same as any gas-chugging car. It's just a longer pollution cycle.

The main point here is that we think of renewable energy as the answer to the problem. Unfortunately, renewables have a long, long journey ahead of them before they are capable of tackling our energy needs *without contributing to the problem*.

Not to mention that there's an aspect to all of this that often goes unnoticed—or is willfully ignored—the excessive energy consumption of servers. In a digital age where streaming services like Netflix have become a staple in American households, servers play a crucial role in delivering our favorite movies and TV shows.

These servers act as electromagnets and consume a tremendous amount of energy.[10] In fact, the data centers that house these servers are some of the fastest-growing consumers of electricity in the world.

There are a few reasons why servers consume so much energy. First, they need a lot of power to run the processors and memory that store and process data. Second, they need to be kept cool, which requires a lot of energy for cooling systems. Third, they often run at full capacity 24/7, which means that they are always consuming energy.

It's important to recognize that while we all focus on the impact of fossil fuel dependence on the environment, the energy consumption of servers is a significant contributor to our overall energy usage. As we indulge in streaming our favorite shows, we should be aware of the environmental cost associated with it.

This is the ugly side of climate change discourse. We don't talk about all the factors. We only talk about the popular ones—rather than the issue as a whole—because there seems to be a certain amount of ignorance about where we're at with this issue.

It's a massive problem to solve that involves our entire societal structure. Don't get me wrong, I have faith in human ingenuity. I believe we can solve the climate change issue and use our innovation, resilience, and resourcefulness to power the world differently with technology we haven't seen yet.

People like Elon Musk are a great source of inspiration to me in this regard. He's moved the needle forward with a sustainable solution that meets the needs of today, but even he knows that it's not perfect. Climate change is real and "we shouldn't be complacent about changing the chemical constituency of our atmosphere and oceans," he said. "If people keep pushing hard, humanity will solve the sustainable energy problem in time."[11]

He's right.

Here's the thing, though—you can use the issue to your advantage. How?

First, let's understand how energy affects our economy and why it matters for your investment portfolio.

Let's look at some basic facts and figures together.

As discussed, it's not feasible to rely solely on renewable energy sources like solar, wind, nuclear, or hydro (water) options. Therefore, nearly all of our energy—from how you keep the heat on at home to filling your car up at the gas station—is derived from fossil fuels.

Fossil fuels—coal, oil, and natural gas—are mined from deep in the earth and processed to create gasoline, diesel fuel, jet fuel, and other petroleum products. There are many terms bandied about, but you'll hear *crude oil* and *petroleum* very frequently. *Crude oil* is the raw substance mined from the earth.[12] *Petroleum* is a broader term for energy products made from crude oil—including crude oil itself.[13]

In 2022, the United States used about 20.28 million barrels of petroleum daily, totaling nearly 7.4 billion barrels over the entire year.[14] Each barrel is 42 gallons.

According to Chevron, one barrel of crude oil can produce:

- Enough liquefied gasses (such as propane) to fill 12 small (14.1 ounces) cylinders for home, camping, or workshop use.
- Enough gasoline to drive a medium-sized car (17 miles per gallon) over 280 miles.
- Asphalt to make about one gallon of tar for patching roofs or streets.
- Lubricants to make about a quart of motor oil.
- Enough distillate fuel to drive a large truck (five miles per gallon) for almost 40 miles. If jet fuel fraction is included, that truck can run nearly 50 miles.
- Nearly 70-kilowatt hours of electricity at a power plant are generated by residual fuel.
- About four pounds of charcoal briquettes.
- Wax for 170 birthday candles or 27 wax crayons.[15]

But there is so much more that comes from petroleum products—more than you might expect. The following is an incomplete list:

- Soaps—Dishwashing liquid, detergents, shampoo
- Personal hygiene products—Deodorant, toothbrushes, toothpaste, shaving cream

- Home essentials—Trash bags, mops, ice cube trays, insect repellant, bandages, shower curtains, TV cabinets
- Durable medical equipment—Sunglasses/eyeglasses, safety glasses, hearing aids, heart valves, prosthetic limbs
- Home improvement products—Floor wax, vinyl flooring, house paint, insulation, roofing, paint brushes/rollers, water pipes
- Cosmetics—Lipstick, hand lotion, cold cream, nail polish, hair dyes, perfume
- Tech—cell phones, keyboards, monitors, laptops, cameras
- Medications—Aspirin, antihistamines, cortisone, antiseptics, petroleum jelly (Vaseline)
- Cloth products—Clothing, backpacks, upholstery fabric, yarn, purses, pajamas, pantyhose, umbrellas
- Plastics—toys, roller skate wheels, hula hoops, ballpoint pens, drinking cups, credit cards
- Sports products—golf balls, footballs, golf bags, kayaks, fishing lures, tennis rackets, skis, swimming pools, tents, skateboards
- Loudspeakers

- Vitamin capsules
- Life jackets
- Guitar strings
- Movie film
- Rubbing alcohol
- Solar panels (!!)[16]

The complete list has over *6,000 products on it.* The reach of fossil fuels is tremendous, beyond the wildest of imaginations.

As you might guess, the future is bright for fossil fuels. We're not breaking up with them any time soon. (I'd like to see you try going without your toothpaste!)

Globally, we use more and more energy—in its various forms—every year, and we produce more and more fossil fuel-dependent products every year, too.[17]

Current estimates predict that fossil fuel energy demand will increase by 47% in the next 30 years, even with the assumption that technology and innovation will make renewable energy a much more realistic option than it is today.[18]

That's nuts to think about—that even as better solutions become more and more viable, fossil fuels will likely still be king.

As we contemplate the persistent dominance of fossil fuels and their ever-growing demand, it's clear that petroleum takes center stage within the energy landscape. Fossil fuels retain their pivotal role, with petroleum drawing particular attention due to its intricate pricing dynamics.

I want to focus on petroleum for another reason, too—it is a prime investment opportunity that many are missing. As a nature lover, I don't enjoy seeing the forecasts about increased petroleum needs and dire climate predictions. As an investor, I see an opportunity.

Petroleum is a great investment for several reasons, the first of which is that the price does not follow the same laws as other assets.

The price of petroleum is not governed by a single formula, but instead arises from a complex interplay of numerous variables. Among these, supply and demand are fundamental—but they are just the tip of the iceberg. Geopolitical tensions, technological innovations, environmental regulation, and market sentiment all contribute to the price fluctuations we witness.

We can't talk about petroleum prices without mentioning the Strategic Petroleum Reserve (SPR). The SPR is maintained by the United States to manage supply disruptions and stabilize prices. This stockpile can be strategically tapped to release oil into the market, aiming to lower prices during crises. However, it's important to recognize that the SPR has its limits—it cannot be the panacea for all supply-related challenges.

The SPR is a major player in America's energy landscape. Both Democratic and Republican administrations have relied on it for decades. Historically, the SPR has served as a vital energy safety net, shielding American families and businesses in the aftermath of natural disasters and mitigating the impacts of geopolitical events that disrupt crude oil markets.

One of the biggest factors in petroleum pricing, however, is inflation. In inflationary times the price of oil is high—much like everything else—but does well because it is a necessity. As demonstrated above, there is almost nothing in your life that is untouched by a barrel of oil.

It's old advice, but it's still good. Owning a piece of inflation is the key to beating it. If you invest in something that tends to do particularly well in inflationary times, you have more of a cushion to protect yourself. Traditionally, commodities, real estate, and gold are great hedges against inflation, too.

The cost of fueling your home or filling up your tank fluctuates constantly. But if you own some stock in Exxon Mobil, they can help you pay your bills. It's kind of wild to think about. You pay at the pump, but they pay you back for it—partially, at least. This means that as times get tough you have something to take the edge off.

It's also worth mentioning that the SPR's current levels raise concerns about its capacity to act as an effective safety net for major emergencies, particularly when compared to its historical reserves before the drawdowns last year. While the current administration has taken steps to refill the SPR, the pace has been relatively modest. The option to employ emergency drawdowns to address surging crude oil prices remains open and unresolved, making it an excellent time to invest.[19]

As the issue remains unresolved, prices will only rise, especially since the SPR is currently down 22% from a year ago and down nearly 50% from its average inventory.[20]

The second reason petroleum is a great investment is because it's unpopular.

When there is an overarching narrative (whether it be about climate change or anything else), my investor brain naturally wants to check out the other side of things because I know that there's often a good opportunity hidden in unpopular things.

Obviously, this is not always the case, but it's always worth a look around to see what potential the unpopular side has to offer. You may discover the next Google.

This is what I mean when I say question the status quo. If there's a big wave on the horizon, you should wonder what's beyond it.

That doesn't mean that you should look down on the

current state of affairs. Two things can be true at the same time—the climate can be threatened AND you can make money off of "evil" oil barrels.

Plus, with the rapid rise of Environmental, Social and Governance (ESG) investing—prioritizing environmental, corporate, and social issues to make investment decisions—fossil fuels are undervalued and underinvested. Pension plans don't usually include fossil fuel investments either, and this makes them relatively cheap and ripe for a return on investment.

One of my favorite investments in this area is Texas Pacific Land Corporation (TPL). As one of the largest landowners in the state of Texas, TPL operates on two fronts. They manage oil and gas royalties from land they own in the Permian Basin and they manage water supply, treatment, disposal, and tracking to aid mining/fracking activities over their land. We'll talk more about TPL later in this book.

It's important to remember that all of this could change with one amazing technological advancement that opens the door for incredible problem solving. The next Elon Musk, so to speak. We just have to keep our eyes peeled and invest in him (or her) before they become overvalued.

Until that point, let's talk about one of the most basic investing tools—bonds.

CHAPTER 8

A BANQUET OF CONSEQUENCES:

How Shaky Markets Destabilize the Safest Investments

"In investing, what is comfortable is rarely profitable."

— Robert Arnott

You might have noticed that my list of inflation-proof investments in the last chapter was suspiciously missing something important—bonds.

While it's true that bonds are historically a great way to beat inflation, I left them out of the last chapter because I wanted to give them the attention they deserve. That's because bonds can be more complicated than you might think.

Bonds are often viewed as a win-win. Since the government spends more on average than it receives in taxes, it needs a way to fund social programs, infrastructure projects, and—if need be—war. Investors loan their money to the government for a fixed period and accrue interest until the bond matures, at which point the money they loaned originally is returned to them.

This is the reason that bonds have been considered the foremost "risk-free" investment in the United States for quite a long time. *Have some cash lying around? Buy some bonds—you can't lose. Want to make some money on the side? Buy a bond—you'll be fine.*

The problem in recent years has been that safety has become less and less guaranteed as the economy changes. Although it's widespread knowledge that bonds are a risk-free investment, it's not quite as well known that you can actually lose money on bonds if you make the right mistakes.

To understand this, let's look at the history of bonds in the United States. Although bonds have been traced back to ancient history, government bonds as we know them today were born during World War I.[1]

Knowing that printing money to pay for war—as both the Confederate and Union states had done during the Civil War—caused tremendous inflation and devaluation of the currency, Treasury Secretary William G. McAdoo was determined to support the war effort without printing more money.[2] Under his direction the Federal Reserve and the U.S. Treasury created the Liberty Bond to finance the United States' entrance into World War I.

Liberty Bonds were available for purchase starting at $50, approximately two weeks of wages for the average factory worker.[3]

Obviously, investing two weeks of wages was nearly

unthinkable for a large portion of the country. Liberty Bonds could be purchased over time—in installments of 25 cents—to resolve this issue.[4]

McAdoo also appealed to the nation's patriotism to drive bond purchases. "We must be willing to give up something of personal convenience, something of personal comfort, something of our treasure—all, if necessary, and our lives in the bargain, to support our [n]oble sons who go out to die for us," he announced to the public.

Ultimately, Liberty Bonds raised $17 billion for the war effort, which covered about two-thirds of the cost.[5] Another $8.8 billion was collected from taxes. Twenty million individuals had purchased Liberty Bonds by the war's end—a staggering number considering the United States only had 24 million households at the time.[6]

Liberty Bonds had a thirty-year maturity date but could be called—or sold to another investor—at fifteen years post-purchase.[7] The Federal Reserve ran four drives over the course of World War I to encourage people to buy bonds. Interest rates varied over time, but the highest return was 4.25% during the final two drives.

The cool thing about Liberty Bonds was that they opened the investing world to people who had never considered it. Previously, investing was seen as a practice for the very wealthy or Wall Street professionals.[8] However, the introduction of the Liberty Bond showed everyday

Americans—from factory workers to farmers—how they could make their money work double time.

War bonds were also issued during the Second World War, and they were converted into savings bonds when the war ended.[9] Savings bonds still exist today. There are several different types of savings bonds available for purchase, all with varying terms and conditions. Generally speaking, if you hold the bond until maturity, you will make your money back—plus some interest—depending on the interest rate at the time of issuance.

Granted, that's much smaller than the potential returns you can get with a good investment in the stock market, but slow, steady, guaranteed returns have their place, too. Historically, bonds are less lucrative than the stock market.[10] For most of the 20th century stocks dominated bonds as a way to invest—both in popularity and yield. Although bonds gained more strength at the beginning of this century, stocks returned to their throne about ten years later.

Some bonds allow you to sell them to other investors before they mature. You buy a bond directly from the U.S. government, but in theory you could buy a bond from someone who needs to sell theirs on what's known as the secondary market. Usually, one would sell off a bond at market price—which might differ from the face value—or the amount the bond was purchased for originally.[11]

And this is how you can make risky bond investments,

even though you're dealing with one of the most impervious investments in human history.

Here's the deal—bonds indicate the economy's health, specifically with inflation. That's because bond yields—or the annual rate of return an investor realizes from the investment based on its face value and interest rate (known as its coupon)—run parallel to interest rates.[12] As my partner, Peter Lacey likes to say: bonds are the price of money.

Therefore, when inflation is high, the Federal Reserve attempts to curb the rising prices by increasing interest rates. This makes money more expensive to borrow, which cuts spending and calms the market. But bonds retain the rate of return from the date of purchase because they have a fixed interest rate.

If for some reason one has to sell a bond off early, they must sell the bond on the secondary market for less than they purchased it (known as a discount to par).

The opposite is true as well. When interest rates are low, selling a bond with a higher yield will result in the bond being sold at a much higher price than its face value—this is known as a premium to par.

This isn't much of an issue if you hold a bond to maturity. The waves of bond yields rise and fall constantly—just like the rest of the economy—but you will ultimately get your money back when the bond matures, regardless of other economic factors. However, if you have to sell your bonds off early, you might get significantly less than you paid if inflation is high.

Nothing illustrates this concept quite as well as recent events. In March 2023, the entire country watched in shock as Silicon Valley Bank (SVB) collapsed in the largest bank failure since 2008. Over the span of two days, clients panicked and withdrew their funds en masse once the bank announced that it needed $2.25 billion to sustain its balance sheet.[13] As interest rates rose in the months preceding, clients needed more liquidity and began withdrawing funds from the bank. As borrowing and buying become more expensive, corporations and individuals need to free up more cash.

However, SVB had most of its money tied up in long-term, low-yield treasury bonds, which they had to sell at a huge loss when more and more customers came clambering for their money.[14]

Originally, SVB's bond portfolio totaled nearly $21 billion with an interest rate of 1.79%, but since interest rates had risen dramatically to curb the post-Covid inflation they were forced to incur a $1.8 billion loss.[15]

Although they tried to close the gap, their attempts to raise capital with stock sales ultimately failed. Investors were spooked, and the bank went into receivership. SVB customers were mainly tech startups—such as Roku, Block-Fi, and Circle—each with millions of dollars held at the bank.[16]

They were ultimately bailed out by the government, who decided to reimburse companies who stood to lose much more than just the $250,000 that the Federal Deposit Insurance Corporation (FDIC) guarantees.

The collapse of SVB and the subsequent government bailout serve as a hefty reminder of the intertwined nature of bond investments and the national debt. As the government stepped in to reimburse companies affected by the bank's failure, it added to the already mounting national debt. As it stands, the over $32 trillion in national debt is made up mostly (about 78%) of the amount of outstanding bonds that the public have loaned to the government.

In other words, most of our national debt is held by the public.[17] Should the government default on its debt (which is unlikely, but certainly possible), you—the bondholder—will lose your money.

The general advice for any portfolio is to hold 60% equity (stocks) and 40% bonds. However, with artificially low interest rates from the Federal Reserve, this ratio performed pretty poorly in 2022 by declining 16%.[18] It's possible that this ratio might not work as well as it used to in the past. We'll see what the future holds for these portfolios.

It's also worth noting that generally—in times of high inflation and debt—bonds tend to perform poorly in comparison to the stock market. There's a line that is oft-quoted that seems appropriate here. Simply put, "inflation is indiscriminate, remorseless, and merciless." Inflations, recessions, and all-around bad monetary policy can make even the "safe" investments risky. We've never been in our current national debt situation, and so there's no way to know what's on the other side of this—especially when it comes to money loaned to the government.

The truth is, it's not likely that you'll lose $1.8 billion in bond investments. If you end up having to sell off a long-term bond early, your losses won't be quite as dramatic thanks to the generally low rate of return that bonds generate. However, Silicon Valley Bank's collapse is an important lesson in diversification.

You can't put all (or even most) of your eggs in one basket. Doing so invites huge risk—even with one of the world's safest investments. The crazy thing is, this isn't novel advice. Everyone knows this, and still, individuals and corporations alike make this mistake all the time.

One might convince themselves that a certain investment is solid, so they simply double down instead of expanding their horizons. Or, they might be extremely risk-averse and only willing to invest in one thing. But the truth is that the more you can spread your money, the better off you are. There is safety in numbers.

Take legendary investor H. Wayne Huizenga, for example. He made his fortune in just about every industry you can think of—"garbage hauling, video rentals, automobile sales and rentals, security alarms, professional sports franchises, hotels, portable toilets, lawn care, bottled water, pest control, billboards, and machine parts washing service."[19]

You may also remember from earlier, his investments included Blockbuster and AutoNation, professional sports teams such as the Miami Dolphins (NFL), Florida Marlins (MLB) and the Florida Panthers (NHL), Republic Waste, and Boca Resorts. It doesn't get more diverse than that

Huizenga had a taste for companies with recurring income and needed stellar customer service to beat the competition. He put his heart and soul into many of his investments, often presiding over the companies, overseeing their operations, and focusing on improving customer relationships.

"In each business," he noted in an interview, "there was a customer service aspect that could be improved. My approach has always been to keep the customer happy. The opportunity for customer service in [the] waste collection [industry] was to pick up the trash at the same time each week and to use clean trucks and equipment. At AutoNation, it was the one-price, no-hassle selling process."[20]

Huizenga was very highly regarded, especially in Florida where he lived for most of his life. Personally, he's one of my investing role models. He displayed common sense, kept his eyes open for promising opportunities, and was unafraid to take intentional risks when the occasion arose. He was a man of his word and a very charitable individual, giving millions to fund cancer research, church programs, and youth programs.[21]

When Huizenga passed away in 2018, he was remembered as a man of unwavering integrity who was known for his astonishing generosity. "He was incredibly generous financially, one of the kindest individuals I've met," said Rev. Richard Anderson, the former senior pastor of Palm City Presbyterian Church where Huizenga and his wife were members.

I'd like to tell you about another investing role model of mine—one you may not have heard of—and his connection with Albert Einstein.

CHAPTER 9

ALBERT EINSTEIN, JOHN TEMPLETON, AND THE POWER OF PATIENCE

"Investing should be more like watching paint dry or grass grow. If you want excitement, take $800 and go to Las Vegas."

— Paul Samuelson

There's a quote famously attributed to Albert Einstein, that says "Compound interest is the eighth wonder of the world. He who understands it, earns it. He who doesn't, pays it." It's not clear whether or not Einstein actually said this, but there's one thing that is clear. In uncertain economic times, you don't want to be paying any more than you have to, so understanding compound interest—and then earning it—is probably the best way to go.

Luckily, you don't have to be a genius like Einstein to understand compound interest.

In essence, compounding allows an investor to earn interest on the principal investment and on the interest already earned from previous periods.[1] Compound interest is interest earned on interest—a system that tacks earned interest onto the principal so that investors earn significantly more over time with compound interest than they would with an investment that only returns simple interest.

For example, imagine you save $10,000 in a bank account with an interest rate of 5% that compounds annually. At the end of year 1, you'll have made 5% on your $10,000, so the balance in the account should be $10,500. At the end of year 2, you'll make 5% on your $10,500, which equals $11,025.00.

After ten years you'll have $16,288.95 in that bank account, provided that you don't spend anything. If you continue to squirrel money away, your bottom line will continue growing.

Compound interest is that friend who knows everyone and keeps bringing new people to the party. As they bring more friends, the party just gets bigger and wilder. It's like a money snowball rolling downhill, growing as it collects more snow. It's a powerful tool, one that you must use to your advantage.

Interest doesn't have to compound annually—it can compound quarterly, monthly, daily, or continually. The more frequent the compounding rate, the more money is added to the snowball—excuse me, the principal. Additionally, compound interest can be found in lots of different investment options, like savings accounts (as in the example above), stocks, bonds, certificates of deposits (CDs), and 401(k) retirement accounts.

The key to compound interest is patience. The longer you can wait, the more money you'll make. Patience is an excellent quality in an investor, for a few reasons.

Patience in investing means carefully choosing investments that you plan to hold for a long time, essentially allowing you to reap the full reward of an excellent investment before you sell it off.

There are some advantages to being a careful, patient investor. Studies show that you're more likely to have a steady income from your investments and less likely to incur extreme losses. Your investments will grow over time and you can give yourself time to think through important decisions before you make them. Investing cautiously gives you the ability to keep your wits about you.[2]

You won't buy stocks on a whim, you'll do your due diligence because you know that you'll likely hold the stock for an extended period of time. Additionally, you'll avoid making rash or emotional decisions based on current popularity or a high selling price.

Longevity decreases your risk across the board—downturns and fluctuations are often temporary. The stock market, overall, has tended to increase in value over time. Even in the case of a dramatic downturn, in the long-term the market has a history of recovery.

In the name of thinking things through clearly, it's worth mentioning that taking the slow lane has disadvantages. You miss opportunities, inflation can cut a chunk out of your bottom line, and cautious investors tend to reap lower returns than expected.[3]

Overall, however, investing patiently and for the long run are much safer, more stable ways to invest than taking the fast lane.

As an example, look at day trading. Over the last few years, day trading has become increasingly more popular. Day trading is essentially buying a stock at the beginning of the day and selling it by the end of the day, hoping that the minor price fluctuations throughout the day will lead to short-term capital gain.

Theoretically, day trading makes sense. Stock prices fluctuate on an hour-to-hour basis, and the fluctuations can be quite severe. If you play your cards right, the winnings can be big.

But that's just it—it's similar to playing cards.

The hourly or daily fluctuations in the stock market are often unpredictable, and minute-to-minute fluctuations are borderline random. You're playing games with your money as a day trader, not investing.

The fact of the matter is that it's hard to make money as a day trader. One study from the University of California found that only 13% of day traders were profitable over a six-month period. Over five years the number of profitable day traders dwindled to 1%.[4] Most profit is eaten up by transaction fees, although there are some day traders who are successful.

In 2020 and 2021, the population of day traders increased significantly.[5] It makes sense. In the early months of the pandemic, we were all home with nothing to do, so why not try your luck on the New York Stock Exchange? It can't hurt.

Well, it can. And you could be using those dollars to invest in something long-term that racks up compound interest and builds your wealth while you sleep.

Warren Buffett is an excellent example of patience in investing. As one of the most successful investors of all time, Buffett has said that the most important quality for an investor is patience. He has backed up this claim by holding onto his investments for long periods of time—most notably the shares of Coca-Cola he bought in 1988 and shares in American Express he bought in 1964. Those investments have paid off handsomely, and Buffett is now one of the wealthiest people on the planet.

I tend to agree with the idea that slow and steady wins the race. Just as driving at the speed limit ensures you a life free from speeding tickets, the same applies here. You will avoid the unforeseen pitfalls and won't get scammed if you invest with hefty doses of thought and patience.

Now you understand patience and compound interest. How do you make it work for you and not against you?

First, you have to know the situations where compound interest is not your friend. When you borrow money—such as with student loans, mortgages, or other personal loans—the longer you take to pay off the debt, the more you will pay. That's because the balance due grows over time as interest compounds.

The same is true for credit cards. The amount you pay monthly is not just the total of all the charges you put on your credit card that month. Instead, it is the total of all charges from that month plus interest compounded over a set period of time. If you fail to pay down the balance regularly, it will simply continue to compound. This will leave you with a huge, yawning hole of debt to fall into.

Not all debt is bad—such as with a mortgage—but it's important that you continually pay your dues so that the debt doesn't balloon out of control. Some people pay their credit card bill or mortgage in two installments a month to mitigate the amount of interest they owe.

If you have student loans or credit card debt, it's important that you know the interest rate and compounding rate so that you can estimate how much the debt will grow if you have to leave it for a period of time.

You can choose, ahead of time, to find loans and credit cards that have a low interest rate or compound less often.

The opposite is true for investments or savings accounts—try to find options with higher interest rates and a more frequent compounding rate.

Another way to make compounding interest work for you is to start early. If you're in your teens when you start to save for retirement, your savings will be much greater than someone who starts thinking about retirement in their 50s—even if you start with a meager amount. Compound interest rewards those who exercise patience and give their investments time to grow.

That's the key—the longer you can wait, the more your money will compound. If you can maximize the amount of periods your money compounds, you're giving yourself a better chance to grow your capital.

No one knew this better than one of the great compounders of our time, Sir John Templeton.

Born in 1912 in Winchester, Tennessee, his middle-class family lost most of their wealth during the Great Depression. Undaunted by hardship, Templeton attended prestigious universities such as Yale and Oxford, financing his tuition with scholarship money, poker winnings, and money from odd jobs.[6]

During his time in college, he was a student of the famed investor and economist Benjamin Graham, who is known as the father of value investing. Value investing is a strategy that encourages buying stocks that appear to be discounted compared to their corresponding worth or intrinsic value.[7] Much of Templeton's investment philosophy was deeply shaped by Graham's value-oriented theories. (Interestingly enough, Warren Buffett also studied under Graham.)

After graduating law school in 1936, Templeton began working on Wall Street for Fenner & Beane. You would likely recognize this company as Merrill Lynch. His indefatigable pursuit of a goal—demonstrated by creatively financing his higher education pursuits—made him a success at the company.

One of the golden rules of the investing world is "buy low, sell high." You've definitely heard that line before, so you're probably aware that it's easier said than done. Buying low and selling high means that you make an investment when it isn't worth much and then sell it off when it's at its zenith to make maximum profit. It can be extremely difficult to pinpoint when the highs are at their highest and the lows are at their lowest, and falling into a herd mentality is all too easy.

Templeton was a whiz at buying low and selling high, and he became very interested in investing in "nations, industries, and companies hitting rock bottom."[8] He was perfectly positioned when the Second World War began in 1939. Templeton—just 26 years old, with $10,000 in his pocket from a loan—bought 100 shares each from 104 companies selling stocks for a dollar or less. He held onto them, and the success was enormous. Only four of the investments failed to turn a profit. After about four years, his portfolio had grown 400%.[9]

Just like Wayne Huizenga, Templeton was a generous philanthropist with key visions for a better future. In 2004, at the age of 92, he gave $50 million to charity. He eventually moved to Nassau, in the Bahamas, and was naturalized as a British citizen. Queen Elizabeth knighted him for his massive impact on the world of philanthropy.[10]

By the time he passed in 2008 at the ripe age of 95, Templeton's portfolio was estimated to be at about $13 billion.[11]

Templeton's "buy low, sell high" strategy required exercising something he called "maximum pessimism"—actively going against the crowd. "It is extremely difficult to go against the crowd—to buy when everyone else is selling or has sold, to buy when things look darkest, to buy when so many experts are telling you that stocks in general, or in this particular industry, or even in this particular company, are risky right now," he explained. "But, if you buy the same securities everyone else is buying, you will have the same results as everyone else. By definition, *you can't outperform the market if you buy the market.* And chances are, if you buy what everyone is buying, you will do so only after it is already overpriced." [12]

Buying low and selling high requires a good bit of

foresight—or so most people think. But Templeton would probably disagree.

Instead, he recognized that the market tends to move cyclically—good times are always around the corner from bad times.[13] With that knowledge, Templeton was able to weather risk at low points and then sell off investments at their highest points. Today this investment strategy is known as a contrarian approach.

Part of Templeton's success was his humility, but another part was his incredible ability to abide by his own investing principles.

He had several rules for investing:

- **Remain flexible.** Notice changing market conditions and adjust your strategy accordingly. "The fact is, there is no one kind of investment that is always best," Templeton noted. "If a particular industry or type of security becomes popular with investors, that popularity will always prove temporary and—when lost—may not return for many years."[14] Therefore, don't get caught in rigid thinking. Instead, be open to adapting your strategies as the world and market evolve.

- **Do your research.** Before taking the plunge, be sure to either do your homework and understand the ins and outs of the investment or hire a capable, experienced expert. Either way, being well-informed will set you up for smarter decisions and help you steer clear of unnecessary risks.

- **Recognize the toll of inflation and taxes.** What will you get out of your investments after taxes and inflation have taken their respective bites? "It is vital that you protect purchasing power," Templeton wrote in 1993. "If inflation averages 4%, it will reduce the buying power of a $100,000 portfolio to $68,000 in just 10 years. In other words, to maintain the same buying power, that portfolio would have to grow to $147,000—a 47% gain simply to remain even over a decade. And this doesn't even count taxes."[15] These numbers are even more drastic today than when he wrote about them. Therefore, make investments that will sustain you even after taxes and inflation, especially for long-term investors.
- **Control your emotions.** Keep your cool—emotions can mess with your investment game. When the market gets crazy, it's tempting to panic and make rash decisions. Emotional decision-making can lead to irrational choices that harm your investment returns. Keep those emotions in check, especially during periods of market volatility.
- **Go bargain hunting**. Search for investments that are high quality at a decent price. Treat the market

like a thrift shop—you'll eventually find something akin to a designer shoe in the discount bin. What is quality when it comes to investments, though? It isn't quite the same as Louis Vuitton or Cartier. According to Templeton, "Quality is a company strongly entrenched as the sales leader in a growing market. Quality is a company that's the technological leader in a field that depends on technical innovation. Quality is a strong management team with a proven track record. Quality is a well-capitalized company that is among the first into a new market. Quality is a well-known trusted brand for a high-profit-margin consumer product."[16]

- **Constantly monitor and review your investments.** Stay in the loop and keep an eye on your investments. Check in regularly to make sure they're still on track with your goals and risk tolerance. Keep up with what's happening in the market, stay informed, and be ready to make adjustments if needed. Being proactive about monitoring your investments helps you make smart moves and adapt to whatever the market throws at you.
- **Invest when you have money.** As the maxim goes, "It is time in the market, not market timing" that determines overall success. In other words, participate

> as soon as you can, and allow time—and patience—to give you a leg up. In the same vein, invest for the long term. "The stock market is not a casino," Templeton pointed out. "But if you move in and out of stocks every time they move a point or two, the market *will* be your casino. And, like most gamblers, you may lose eventually—or frequently."[17]

That last point is the one I want to drive home. A common misconception—one that we've been discussing throughout this book—is that you must invest with the kind of careless zeal of a daredevil. To take a risk you have to be an adrenaline junkie who loves living on the edge. To successfully make money off the market, you have to be faster, stronger, wiser, and braver than anyone else. You must bet everything you have—practically your entire net worth—for the entire venture to be worthwhile.

Those assumptions couldn't be further from the truth. The most successful investors—our Warren Buffett, Wayne Huizenga, and John Templeton exemplars—didn't (and still don't) play by those rules, and you don't have to either.

You can move slower, wait patiently, do your due diligence, and still outstrip everyone else. Slow and steady does in fact win the race. A large part of winning that race is making wise decisions. Once you've made those decisions, compound interest coupled with patience can make a

$20,000 investment well over $100,000 in 30 years—without investing anything else.

My advice as an experienced financial advisor and investor is to embrace the power of patience and compound interest in your investment journey. Remember that moving slowly and deliberately doesn't equate to falling behind—in fact, it can often lead to outperforming others in the long run.

You don't have to be a brilliant mind like Albert Einstein or a natural investor like John Templeton. You just have to know how to use the tools you've been given and learn from the success of others.

CHAPTER 10

CRYPTOCURRENCY:

The Bold and Risky Experiment that Rewrote the Rules of Money

"The biggest mistake investors make is to believe that what happened in the recent past is likely to persist."

— Ray Dalio

Cryptocurrency may still be in its awkward teenage phase, but the sheer potential and raw power it possesses is nothing short of mind-blowing.

If you're rolling your eyes, don't worry. I was once in your camp too.

I learned about crypto—specifically Bitcoin—for the first time in 2011. I was speaking to a few college kids who admitted to me they had been using Bitcoin to buy weed. I thought nothing of it, other than kids were getting creative with their Monopoly money these days.

I'll admit, the assumption that cryptocurrency is fake, a scam, or an illegitimate form of currency stayed with me for a while. It wasn't until recently that I recognized its power. I've spent several years learning more about cryptocurrency and Bitcoin, and I've written two white papers on the subject. I own Bitcoins and a few other cryptos, and I truly feel that it is a major part of the future of our economy.

But first, what is cryptocurrency?

Two disclaimers before we get into the meat of it.

1. For the purposes of this discussion, *we'll only be talking about Bitcoin.* As the first true cryptocurrency, it's considered the most stable and trusted. Additionally, the groundbreaking technologies used with Bitcoin are replicated in other cryptocurrencies, making them easier to understand once you've got the basics of Bitcoin down. It's important to note that while other cryptocurrencies may work similarly, each has significant differences. It's important to do your research about how each cryptocurrency works before investing.

2. For many people, cryptocurrency is an extremely novel concept that involves coding language and other unfamiliar technologies. In that regard, it can be difficult to understand. I've attempted to write about this as clearly as possible to increase the likelihood that the average person will understand the material. You may want to read through this chapter a few times, as well as read through some of

the source material provided at the end of this book for more precise information.

With that out of the way, let's get started.

In essence, cryptocurrency is a form of digital currency that uses cryptographic algorithms to secure transactions and control the creation of new units, or "tokens."[1]

Cryptographic algorithms—cryptography—scramble or "encrypt" sensitive information so that only the intended recipient can access the tokens being sent. To unscramble the information a hacker would need to get his hands on a specific passcode or physical key. When you send crypto to another individual, that transaction is encrypted for security and recorded in a blockchain.

A blockchain is basically a massive public ledger. Information—in this case, transactions—is stored in "blocks." Blocks have maximum storage capacities, so once a block has reached capacity it is closed and linked to the previous block.[2] Thus, it's a chain of blocks. The role of a blockchain is to record and verify transactions.

In review, there are two parts to cryptocurrency—

1. The source code that creates the currency.
2. The blockchain that stores and verifies the transactions of that currency.

It all starts with "miners." Miners are individuals who act as bookkeepers for these transactions, using powerful computers (called nodes) to validate and process them by solving mathematical equations called a "proof of work." Miners verify blocks of transactions and store them in the blockchain. When they do so successfully, they are rewarded with newly-minted tokens. These are automatically released by the source code and recorded on the blockchain as well. Node operators maintain copies of the blockchain to ensure the network remains secure and accurate.

To the casual observer, the process might appear circular and counterintuitive. However, it is vital to maintain the integrity of the Bitcoin network. The miners and nodes play an essential role in authenticating all transactions on the network and thwarting attempts to cheat the system.

By verifying transactions and adding them to the blockchain—and triggering the release of newly-minted Bitcoins—miners create an ironclad, immutable record of all transactions, which provides security and transparency for users of the network.

You can think about all of this in the context of a shared spreadsheet. For example, Google Sheets allows individuals to access, update, maintain and verify information from multiple computers and other devices. As long as the link is shared, anyone can see that spreadsheet. If the spreadsheet is not updated, it becomes useless.

Blockchain technology works similarly, except on a much larger scale and with security implementations in place to prohibit changes to sensitive transaction data that might allow token or identity theft.

Unlike Google Sheets, the blockchain is a public ledger that cannot be easily changed—this helps prevent fraud and theft. By using a network of nodes and miners, Bitcoin can operate independently of any central authority. This is what makes it a unique and innovative form of digital currency.

You might be thinking, "Ok, so what's the big deal?"

As we discussed in previous chapters, much of the financial and economical issues we face today are a direct result of the devaluation of our currency by the federal government and central bank. The policies they have instituted have real—and often disastrous—effects on the value of our dollars and cents.

Third-party verification and control has traditionally been the way we keep our financial establishments safe. However, individuals in those institutions can make mistakes, have ulterior motives, or simply be bad actors. This is essentially eroding the trust we have placed in the institutions they represent.

In contrast, cryptocurrencies—and the blockchain technology that supports them—are completely decentralized.[3] This means that there is no one central entity controlling the issuing of new tokens or the verification of transactions.

Instead, transactions and verifications are recorded and overseen by a large network of users—the miners—who all "sign off"on the validity of the transactions. This is known as a consensus mechanism, and it's aimed at preventing total control by one entity and safeguarding the whole system from a single point of failure.

Bitcoin is not a company—there is no CEO or VP, no Board of Directors or marketing team. Bitcoin is an open source code, meaning that anyone can see, copy, change, and distribute its code free of cost.[4] To make changes to the code, however, proposed edits must be reviewed and agreed upon by most participants in the network—not a simple feat.

Crypto is the hottest thing on the market right now because it completely changes how we access, use, store, and think about money. It breaks all the traditional rules once considered to be indisputable and will change the face of our economy as we know it—in my humble opinion, in an extremely positive way.

The idea of cryptocurrency was bandied about at the beginning of the internet era but did not become a reality until January 3, 2009, when the Bitcoin source code was made public and available for use.[5] Satoshi Nakamoto is credited with the creation of Bitcoin, although to this day no one knows who he is.

There are many theories about his identity, although most generally assume that the moniker "Satoshi Nakamoto" is a pseudonym. Some believe he is a group of programmers under a single name rather than an individual. Regardless, Nakamoto mentioned in an email that he was moving away from Bitcoin in 2010, and no one has heard from him since.[6] He is presumed dead.[7]

Nakamoto solved the biggest problem that cryptocurrency faced in its infancy—double-spend.[8] Unlike physical currency, digital currency can be replicated. Just like you can copy and paste paragraphs or links, digital currency can be—for lack of a better term—copied and pasted, and the same tokens can be used in multiple transactions. You simply can't spend the same dollar twice, but with intangible digital currency you certainly can.

By introducing the blockchain concept, Nakamoto resolved the double-spend problem—without using the traditional third-party verification process. With a blockchain, timestamping, encryption, and validation happens over a network of thousands of computers. This makes it nearly impossible for a single entity to gain control over large swaths of the system or replicate tokens.

Since its inception 13 years ago, Bitcoin has never been hacked.

Additionally, it is the only monetary system that can

accurately claim that it has never circulated counterfeit currency.[9]

It may sound too good to be true, and there are some significant risks to Bitcoin and other cryptocurrencies that need to be acknowledged.

As a decentralized and unregulated form of currency, cryptocurrencies do not have the same legal protections as credit cards or bank accounts.[10] Although the Bitcoin algorithm has never been hacked, other cryptocurrencies have been and individuals' wallets have been accessed and stolen. Unfortunately, there is no way to get that money back. The same goes for transactions made with cryptocurrency—they are usually irreversible.

Moreover, cryptocurrencies tend to have massive and dramatic fluctuations in value and do not have a well-established history of rebounding.

Furthermore, fraudulent and misleading companies are rampant, cheating people out of their hard-earned money. It's essential to thoroughly research a cryptocurrency company before deciding to invest.

Still, Bitcoin and other cryptocurrencies are an excellent way to diversify your portfolio without biting off more than you can chew.

We'll speak about this more in the next chapter.

For now, cryptocurrency illustrates the creative, unorthodox thinking I spoke about in the previous chapter.

Recognizing the inherent flaws of our international third-party banking system, cryptocurrencies seek to rectify those issues—by completely breaking the rules. The reshaping of our financial systems is happening before our eyes, and it is pretty marvelous to watch.

It also takes a fearless, open-minded investor to take the first jump into cryptocurrencies. The payoff is enormous. Nakamoto is said to hold around 1 million Bitcoins—if he is alive, he is a multi-billionaire. I see fantastic returns with clients of mine who were willing to take the risk, too.

So, how do you capitalize on some of that yourself? Why is buying and holding Bitcoin important, even if you're not convinced of its worth? How do you do it safely?

We'll talk about it all in the next chapter. Don't shut the book yet.

CHAPTER 11

THE RISE OF DIGITAL GOLD:

Why Investing in Crypto is the Future

"I could either watch it happen or be a part of it."
— Elon Musk

If you think I'm crazy for encouraging clients to invest in cryptocurrency—especially as unregulated, volatile, and thorny as it is—hear me out.

Imagine this. You're a Jew in Nazi Germany—you've been stripped of your business, degrees and certifications, home, and finally, citizenship. It's only a matter of time before they come for your money, too.

And they do. In 1938 Jews in Germany and Austria were required to register any property or assets worth more than 5,000 Reichsmarks with the German government—that's equivalent to about $34,000 today.[1] As time passed, Jews increasingly lost tax incentives for having children or owning property and were placed in the highest income bracket, regardless of their actual income.

Additionally, Jews were accused of tax evasion, and

many Jewish businesses were required to pay tax debts they did not owe. To legally leave Germany at the time, one had to surrender over 50% of their assets.

Jews leaving Germany—lawfully or otherwise—were strategically divested of their wealth, regardless of whether they had much of it.

Back then wealth was measured in physical money, gold, valuable artwork, and property. And it's pretty hard to load up a van full of gold, paintings, or money and try to get it out of Nazi Germany without anyone noticing. You certainly can't take your mansion with you, either.

For all of human history, wealth has mainly manifested in physical money or value. As empires rose and fell—from Rome to Nazi Germany—people's wealth came and went with it, from the richest to the poorest.

It's true to this day. Your money is tied to the economic wellness of the country you live in—your ability to make it, keep it, invest it, and exchange it for equal value depends on a host of unique factors. The biggest of these factors being the place you call home.

Crypto changes all of this.

Cryptocurrencies are stored in a digital wallet (a hot wallet) or offline in a small USB thumb drive (a cold wallet), so you can take your money anywhere. Anyone with an internet connection can buy, sell, exchange, and access crypto. It's secure and frictionless, so you don't have to wait until 9 AM to access it like you would with a bank.

Crypto has no nationality—it can be transferred anywhere—making it the first-ever universal store of value. Since a singular third party does not control it, inflationary monetary policies or growing national debt will not devalue your crypto. It's impossible to confiscate without shutting down the Internet. Plus, Bitcoin's source code only allows for 21 million tokens to be released, making it a scarce commodity that is likely to increase in value. (Other cryptocurrencies have similar scarcity measures in place.)

And while every transaction is recorded and published in a very public blockchain, sensitive information such as your name or address are not available to even the most sophisticated hackers.

For me, this is the reason why Bitcoin is so important.

I'm not suggesting that the United States is about to go rogue on its own population and Constitution, as in Nazi Germany. I don't know what the future holds. But for those who are concerned about the stability of the global financial system—with its foundation firmly placed in the health and welfare of the United States economy—cryptocurrency is a very attractive (partial) solution. And for those who live in countries that want to control their every move, crypto is tyranny-proof. Crypto is freedom from oppression.

It's the 21st Century version of stuffing money under the mattress for a rainy day—but instead of sitting there possibly losing value, your dollars (exchanged for tokens) go up in value. You're taking money off the grid and investing it at the same time. You're making sure no one controls your money but yourself, which is a security that previous generations were not privileged enough to have.

Let's dive further into the significant risks that come with cryptocurrency that we mentioned in the previous chapter.

The lack of regulation is a double-edged sword—it gives crypto the raw power to change how we handle money fundamentally, but it also opens the door to people just waiting for the right moment to take all of it. Crypto is the wild West of our current economy—there is colossal potential to strike it rich with (digital) gold, but enough bandits and thieves out there to make it a risky endeavor.

The industry is full of bad actors, like Sam Bankman-Fried and his now-bankrupt FTX cryptocurrency/exchange. The cryptocurrency entrepreneur founded two companies—Alameda Research and FTX—in 2017 and 2019 respectively. Alameda Research, a crypto-based quantitative trading firm, and FTX, a crypto exchange firm, took off in the beginning of the pandemic when crypto made front and center in the financial industry. By 2020, FTX had acquired another exchange company, Blockfolio, and its client base continually increased. FTX acquired several other (failing) crypto companies in the following years, appearing to be a stable, well-established company amidst a volatile crypto industry.[2]

However, on November 2, 2022, rumors spread that most of FTX's cash was in the form of its own crypto token, FTT. The news prompted several major companies to announce that they were selling their FTT tokens—this prompted a massive fall in FTT's price and a major liquidity problem for FTX.

A rival exchange—Binance—announced intent to buy FTX, but "after a day of due diligence, Binance opted out. [Binance CEO Changpeng] Zhao shared that the financial situation was too dire for a cost-effective fix."[3] In their announcement, Binance noted that the rational for backing out of the deal was "mishandled customer funds and alleged U.S. agency investigations."[4]

Reports of mishandled customer funds brought the SEC out to investigate. By November 11, 2022, Bankman-Fried resigned as CEO and both FTX and Alameda Research declared bankruptcy.[5]

It became clear that Bankman-Fried had "transferred at least $4 billion from FTX to Alameda Research…after his trading firm suffered losses on crypto deals."[6] The transferred money included customer funds. The two companies were closely tied, lending money to one another and propping each other up.[7] On December 13, 2022, the SEC charged

Bankman-Fried with "orchestrating a scheme to defraud equity investors."[8]

In a press release, the SEC wrote:

"Bankman-Fried orchestrated a years-long fraud to conceal from FTX's investors (1) the undisclosed diversion of FTX customers' funds to Alameda Research LLC, his privately-held crypto hedge fund; (2) the undisclosed special treatment afforded to Alameda on the FTX platform, including providing Alameda with a virtually unlimited 'line of credit' funded by the platform's customers and exempting Alameda from certain key FTX risk mitigation measures; and (3) undisclosed risk stemming from FTX's exposure to Alameda's significant holdings of overvalued, illiquid assets such as FTX-affiliated tokens."[9]

To make matters worse, he "used commingled FTX customers' funds at Alameda to make undisclosed venture investments, lavish real estate purchases, and large political donations."[10]

Understandably, such fiascos make crypto a target for blanket federal regulation, which would blunt the industry's power and completely undermine the purpose of crypto. Obviously, irresponsible and lawless people—like Sam Bankman-Fried—must be stopped. But the question remains: how do you do that without cutting the industry off at its knees?

It's still unclear what jurisdiction the Securities and Exchange Commission has over cryptocurrency exchanges, although SEC Chairman Gary Gensler has announced that "The law is clear. If you're a securities exchange, clearinghouse, broker, or dealer, you must come into compliance, register with us, deal with conflicts of interest, and disclose important information. For 90 years, these laws have helped protect investors like you."[11]

Exchanges such as Coinbase balk at the idea of regulation under the existing SEC framework, as they believe that crypto is a unique and novel asset that must have a completely new framework for regulation.

There's no clear answer to this problem yet.

Crypto has become an increasingly popular investment, especially by the masses. In other parts of this book I caution against going with the crowd, instead taking a contrarian approach. In the name of being totally upfront and honest, this is also a factor you must consider when investing in crypto. Although Bitcoin is hardly the newest token—and most definitely the most secure one—its rise in popularity is concerning due to inflated value and the possibility of a bubble, which is something we'll discuss in the next chapter.

For the time being, however, let's leave it at this: crypto is complex, so I encourage you to be cautious. I recommend

Bitcoin above all other tokens—mainly for its stability, security, and cutting-edge technology—but Bitcoin still comes with risks. The inherent volatility, uncertainty, and instability of all crypto make it an investment you must take in small bites. Therefore, I don't believe you should make crypto a significant part of your investment portfolio. Consider making it between 1% and 5% of your portfolio, depending on your risk tolerance.

This may seem obvious to some, but play by the rules as they apply to you. The IRS considers crypto "property," so if you buy, sell, or exchange crypto, you must report that on your taxes.[12] Do your due diligence and speak to your accountant about how to do so when tax time comes around.

It's also worth mentioning that crypto isn't the only hedge against inflation, as we discussed in previous chapters. It's simply the most groundbreaking one, and the one with the most pure potential to change everything we know about our financial system. Classically, other excellent hedges against inflation are collectables—art, stamps, vintage items, antique cars—as well as precious metals like gold and silver.

These kinds of investments work as a buffer between your money and the open, hungry mouths of inflation monsters because they don't lose their value based on monetary fluctuations. Instead, they retain value due to their scarcity—as well as their practical use—as in the case of precious metals.

But I digress. Back to crypto.

As I mentioned, do thorough research before investing in cryptocurrency. Bitcoin is just the beginning. Thousands of other tokens are out there, and I don't think every token available is worth your time or money.

When you're looking to invest in a specific token, ask yourself honestly:

- Why am I doing this? Am I getting caught up in the hype?
- Does this seem too good to be true?
- Do I understand how this cryptocurrency operates? What parts don't I understand?
- Am I properly set up to safely store the tokens I purchase?
- How much can I afford to lose?
- What's my exit strategy?

Just like other investments, crypto is a patience game. The wild ups and downs can cause massive losses for short-term investors. Some cryptos have not returned from the dead, so the potential for loss is steep.

However, the overall trend for Bitcoin over the past 13

years has been highly positive—which is one of the reasons I prefer Bitcoin over other tokens.

I truly believe that Bitcoin is the future of our currency. Our world gets increasingly smaller as globalization continues, which leaves little room for economic error. Look at the Great Depression—it began in the United States and spread financial difficulty throughout the world, triggering the rise of dictatorial regimes in Germany and Japan and bringing us closer to the devastation of World War II.[13]

We are significantly more interdependent than in the 1930s, so the United States' economic troubles will have ripple effects worldwide. For that reason, many (myself included) feel that crypto is a good option in the face of an ever-tightening noose around our necks. It's independent of all governments and currencies, usable worldwide, easily accessible, and entirely controlled by you.

It's a new way to protect yourself, which is why I believe Bitcoin is such a good investment.

Bitcoin is likely to be a defining asset of our time, similar to the land or gold of previous generations. There will be those who have it and can reap its benefits and those who will not be as fortunate. I encourage you to take advantage of it while you still can.

CHAPTER 12

FRENZY AND FALLOUT:

How Bubbles Inflate and Burst

"In the history of every great catastrophe, you will find that some masterly bit of stupidity sets fire to the oil-soaked rags."

— Edwin Lefevre

Over the course of my career, I've witnessed four major economic bubbles as they rose, grew, and then burst. I've learned important lessons from them—lessons that I actively practice in my day-to-day interactions with clients and my personal investing strategy.

Before I get into the key takeaways, let's take a closer look at each of these bubbles—their origins, the reasons behind why they happened, the way they unfolded, and the lasting impact that remains relevant today.

The first two bubbles of my career were inherently tied to the Iranian Revolution and the subsequent two oil crises of the 70s and 80s.

The first of these was the domestic oil crisis of 1980, and the second was Japan's asset price bubble. We'll talk about the Japanese first.

Known for their innovation and technological prowess, post-World War II Japan was powering its way to the top and dominating the automobile and personal electronics industries. The Japanese economy grew by leaps and bounds in a relatively short period of time.

However, things began to look bleak in 1979 with the second oil crisis. In the midst of the Iranian Revolution global exports of precious oil dropped precipitously, spurring a widespread panic of shortages and high prices.[1] To combat this issue, Japan lowered interest rates.[2]

The rates remained low—and dipped even lower—well into the 1980s.

In 1983, the Nikkei 225 stock index was worth 10,000. Over the next six years, that number would quadruple to a whopping peak of 38,916.

The Japanese economy grew further in 1985, as Japan, France, Germany, the United States, and the United Kingdom agreed on the Plaza Accord—acknowledging the trade deficit between the strong U.S. dollar and the weak Japanese yen (and German Deutsche mark).[3] The solution was to actively depreciate the dollar, strengthening the other two currencies and ultimately leveling the playing field.

However, the rising yen caused a shock to export-based Japanese companies, triggering Japan to expand its monetary policy and boost its economy.

Coupled with land scarcity and a highly speculative

investment scene, these monetary policies caused a massive overvaluation of both stocks and real estate. Real estate and stock prices climbed, climbed, and climbed even higher, until they became unaffordable to most.

By 1988, the theoretical value of land in Japan had surpassed that of all the land in the United States four times over.[4] To put that into perspective, the United States is 25 times larger than Japan. A golf membership could cost millions.[5] The estimated value of a single district in downtown Tokyo was enough to purchase the whole of Canada.

Japan's economy was poised to eat the United States' alive.

Spoiler—it didn't.

The huge rise in cost culled a majority of buyers from the market, significantly dulling demand and stunting the seemingly unlimited growth. As demand fell, the government tightened up its monetary policy to stave off the worst, making money less accessible. However, the higher interest rates weren't enough. As the 90s came around, companies were plunging into bankruptcy, overzealous investors had lost millions, and the job market was nearly nonexistent.[6] Banks and other financial institutions found themselves deep in the red.

The bubble had burst. The party was over.

In its wake was a graveyard of unfinished factories and

real estate projects, rampant unemployment, and bittersweet memories of better times.[7]

The post-bubble period of recession and stagnation is known colloquially as the lost decade.[8] This era—generally understood as lasting from 1990 to 2001—saw the Japanese economy stuck in the mire, growing only at 1.14%. Land value fell by 70%; equity (stock) value dropped 60%.

The lost decade wasn't really a decade, though. It was more like three decades. The fall only bottomed out in 2009, as the Nikkei 225 tumbled to its lowest point at 7,500.[9]

To this day—35 years later—the index has not recovered its previous highs.

Just as Japan was lowering interest rates to keep a recession at bay in the midst of the '79 oil crisis, the United States was experiencing a time of pliant monetary policy as well.

In 1978, the Federal Reserve believed that looser monetary policy would help take down the rising rate of unemployment.[10] However, unemployment rates continued rising, and the Iranian Revolution shut off the oil spigots. The accommodating monetary policy coupled with higher energy prices resulted in an inflationary spike.

By March of 1979 inflation had risen to 7%, and there was growing concern that it would continue to rise. The Federal Reserve attempted to curb inflation with a timid interest rate hike, from 6.9% in 1978 to 10% by year's end.

Just like the Japanese, this move was not aggressive enough and inflation rose to 9% by the beginning of 1980.

Oil prices reached $35 per barrel that year, equivalent to $129.84 in today's dollars.[11] The rapid increase was due to widespread fear of another oil shortage, leading to speculative hoarding.[12] Additionally, demand was high to support the flourishing international economy. However, the oil shortage and subsequent inflation placed the global economy in a recession.

To normalize prices, the global market began looking outside of the politically unstable Middle East for oil—locations such as Siberia, Alaska, and the Gulf of Mexico were explored. Production from non-OPEC sources such as these outpaced OPEC countries by 1981.

American producers found themselves in a prosperous position. The energy industry became the money maker—*the* hot ticket to success.

"Money sloshed around Texas as independent oil producers took out millions in loans to buy the equipment needed to drill from Kilgore to Wichita Falls to Midland. Manpower was needed not just in the oil patch but in the search for petroleum. Geologists, landmen, and attorneys flocked to the state to find the underground reservoirs and to secure the mineral rights needed to drill.

And then there were the banks, jewelers, and car

dealerships that catered to the overnight millionaires.

Real estate soon emerged as the most noteworthy outlet for Texas money. With growth in commerce and in population, it seemed quite logical at the time to invest big in new housing developments, soaring skyscrapers in Dallas and Houston, shopping centers, and vacation condominiums on South Padre Island."[13]

But the party was waning almost as soon as it had begun. Even though the likelihood of another oil shortage was decreasing, prices remained much higher than they had been before the crisis. This made reducing energy consumption an easy way to save money, and many people opted to drive less and use other methods of transportation instead.

Additionally, new standards required that cars achieve a fuel efficiency of at least 22 miles per gallon by the 1982 model year.[14] With the overall reduction in energy usage, oil companies saw a major plunge in demand. Simultaneously, the 80s heralded an all-time high for oil production with the addition of those non-OPEC producers.

As a result, oil prices plunged.

"Widespread recession in industrialized countries and more efficient use of oil have created a world oil surplus and a resulting fall in prices," *The New York Times* announced in 1982.[15] Between 1981 and 1985, prices declined nearly

40%.[16] In 1986, prices almost completely collapsed, falling more than 50%.

At that point, "Oil was priced at $12.51, still high compared with 15 years before," but overzealous Texas oil barons were in trouble.[17] They had over-invested in oil rigs, thinking they would be needed to meet a surge in demand. When demand was far less than they had accounted for, they had to default on their loans—millionaires became bankrupt overnight.

Former Governor of Texas John Connally was one of the more famous bankruptcies at the time. Having accumulated $48 million in debt, he was forced to sell his multiple homes and a lifetime of possessions.[18]

The Washington Post reported at the time that Connally "made no excuses."

"We were trying to move too far too fast," he said. "We were not conservative enough in consolidating our position with each project. But that is hindsight, and even if we had been more cautious, we might have owed a little less money, but we might have ended up at the same place anyway—in bankruptcy court."[19]

Oil prices did not recover to their 80s peak until 2004.

—

The third and fourth bubbles of my career were inherently tied together as well. Nothing happens in a vacuum, and one could argue that these two bubbles were each smaller components of a much larger bubble.

The genesis of this story began in 1998, when Long-Term Capital Management (LTCM), a prominent and highly successful hedge fund suffered a catastrophic collapse. LTCM had heavily relied on a leveraged investment approach that hinged on arbitrage for generating returns. This precarious strategy initially yielded success, but proved unsustainable over the long term. Remarkably, LTCM achieved its peak with reported assets of $5 billion and investment positions that amounted to an estimated $1 trillion just a few short years after its founding in 1994.[20]

The poison pill, however, was that a substantial portion of their portfolio consisted of Russian government bonds. In the aftermath of the Soviet Union's dissolution, Russia's economy endured a period of hardship. Russia made several economic reforms in an effort to stabilize the economy, but the adjustment was still "marked by a prolonged transitional depression and macroeconomic instability: seven years of continuing decline [ultimately] result[ing] in a cumulative GDP drop of more than 40% between 1989 and 1996."[21]

The problems were stacked against Russia—it had inherited foreign debt from the former Soviet Union, was plagued with "large-scale tax evasion and huge private capital flight," and had a lack of "fiscal discipline" as the government ran up huge budget deficits financed by the central bank.[22]

Despite that, 1997 saw a brief rise in foreign investments. Negotiations to pay down the inherited debt—as well as relaxed regulations on foreign investments—made Russia an appealing opportunity.

But just as things were looking up, it all fell apart. The Asian Financial Crisis—triggered by the collapse of the Thai Baht—spooked investors in the summer of 1997. Russia's financial shortcomings were open wounds, festering from the Asian crisis as commodity prices fell and caused a steep deterioration in Russia's terms of trade.[23] "The cumulative fall in terms of trade amounted to about 25% from mid-1997 to mid-1998, an annualized cost to Russia's balance of payments of more than $20 billion, nearly one-fourth of exports," the International Monetary Fund wrote.[24]

The situation became unsustainable, and Russia defaulted on its debts on August 17, 1998. The Russian Ruble lost two-thirds of its value over the course of three weeks.[25] LTCM took a huge hit, preparing to default on its own loans. However, the U.S. government feared that the failure of LTCM would set off a massive financial crisis because LTCM's creditors would be forced to write off over $4 billion in debt.[26]

The U.S. government made two moves. The first move was to bail out LTCM with a loan of $3.65 billion, allowing them to liquidate and dissolve by 2000. The federal bailout of LTCM was the first of its kind—an unprecedented move that would be repeated in the future with disastrous consequences.

The second move was to cut interest rates, flooding the market with excess liquidity—much of which found its way back to the stock market.[27]

The hottest new thing on the stock market in those days was Internet-based companies. People were feverishly showering internet startups with money in the hopes of them turning a profit.[28] Many "bet the ranch," on the Internet without heeding the elementary (and cautionary) principles of investing, mostly out of fear of being left behind. Investors "freely invested in any company with a '.com' after its name."[29]

It was a frenzy—companies went public without any "revenue, profits, and, in some cases, a finished product," and still somehow saw their stock prices rise threefold or fourfold in a single day.[30] The Nasdaq rocketed up 5x between 1995 and 2000, reaching a peak of 5,048.62 in March of 2000.[31]

At the beginning of the decade, "the value of stocks traded on the Nasdaq was 11% of the value of stocks traded on the New York Stock Exchange." By the end of the decade, "the market value of Nasdaq was 80% of stocks traded on the NYSE."[32]

But investors weren't the only ones causing a rapid rise in value. Startups—with money flowing in from every direction—felt the pressure to get big and turn a profit, fast. Many companies did not have a workable business model, lacked proprietary technology, and burned through most of their cash on their marketing.[33] Their efforts were spent attempting to set their brand apart from the competition, making them look bigger and more successful than they really were.

Media outlets fed the hysteria, "encourag[ing] people to invest in risky tech stocks by peddling overly optimistic expectations on future returns."[34]

However, the frenzy couldn't sustain itself. The bubble burst in 2002 as the previously unimpeded rising prices rose too high. The excess capital had dried up, resulting in a huge drop in the value of many stocks. In October of that year, the Nasdaq fell 77% from its previous high, to 1,139.90.[35]

A multitude of companies swiftly lost their value, many of which had never recorded a profit. Estimated losses exceeded $5 trillion. While a few notable companies survived (like Microsoft and Netflix), the tech sector was awash in a bloodbath of bankruptcies.

The repercussions of the dot-com bubble reverberated through technology markets worldwide, hurling the international economy into the beginnings of a recession. In typical recession fashion, interest rates fell to stimulate the economy which encouraged borrowing and spending. With Alan Greenspan at its helm, the Federal Reserve slashed interest rates eleven times between 2000 and 2004.[36]

Lower interest rates always mean easy, cheap money—easy, cheap money often mean unsustainable lending practices. The most notable of these practices is the lending of money to subprime buyers—those with poor credit history—to buy homes.

You know where this is going, don't you? With the free and easy lending environment, demand for houses went way through the roof and drove prices even higher. Borrowers jumped to take advantage of the lower interest rates. The subsequent loans were sold to Wall Street as mortgage-backed securities and collateralized debt obligations (CDOs).[37] In fact, when the Nasdaq crashed and Greenspan lowered interest rates in the wake of the dot-com bubble, the money flowed into real estate and increased investment activity in the sector.

Simultaneously, the SEC eased up requirements for the net capital rule that requires "that firms must at all times have and maintain net capital at specific levels to protect customers and creditors from monetary losses that can occur when firms fail."[38]

The new change allowed institutions with over $5 billion in assets—specifically, the big guys like Goldman Sachs, Merrill Lynch, Lehman Brothers, Bear Stearns, and

Morgan Stanley—to leverage their initial investments with almost no limit.[39] During that period it was not unusual to see these institutions leveraging investments by factors as high as 30 or 40 times.[40]

By June of 2004, the market had reached a saturation point. Home ownership reached a peak of 69.2%, and interest rates began to rise incrementally, ultimately reaching 5.25% in 2007.

With rising interest rates, demand fell and prices fell with it.

By 2006, many Americans were in real trouble. Their houses were worth significantly less than what they had paid for them, having bought them at highly inflated prices. If they were struggling with other debt—a real possibility, as many were never in a position to afford a home in the first place—they couldn't sell their home to pay off those debts. The money they would get from the home wouldn't cover the original loan, nor would it cover their debts.

The next year saw the death of subprime mortgage lenders, one after another after another. In the beginning of 2007 alone, more than 25 subprime mortgage lenders declared bankruptcy.[41] The fourth bubble of my career had popped, and it took down the housing market and the highly-leveraged finance sector with it.

The carnage was brutal. It began with Bear Stearns halting redemptions in two of its hedge funds by July of

2007—the first sign of spillover into the finance world. In August, France's BNP Paribas announced that "there [was] no liquidity in the market for the assets held by three of its hedge funds," revealing that the meltdown, and huge investment in mortgage-backed securities, was a global issue.[42] UBS, a Swiss bank, announced that its losses totaled almost $3.4 billion due to subprime mortgage investments.[43]

The Federal Reserve and several other foreign central banks organized and unified to dole out loans to financial institutions facing losses in the trillions, still sorting out the "toxic" investments in their laps.

The United States plummeted into a full-blown recession by 2008. The US government seized control of mortgage lenders Fannie Mae and Freddie Mac, both of which were overrun with mortgage defaults. Major financial institutions fell—starting with Bear Stearns in March and followed by Lehman Brothers that summer. To this day, Lehman Brothers holds the record for the largest bankruptcy filing in U.S. history with $619 billion in debt.[44] While they did not bail out Lehman Brothers, the government bailed out the failing American International Group (AIG) with an $85 billion loan, for fear that AIG's collapse would trigger further collapses in the U.S. and global markets. The move echoed the bailout of LTCM, both companies deemed "too big to fail."

Several other banks failed, including Washington Mutual

and Wachovia.[45] The two largest remaining investment banks—Morgan Stanley and Goldman Sachs—announced that they would convert to bank holding companies. While they would be exposed to more federal regulation, this move allowed them to access more federal funding. This "mark[ed] the end of independent investment banks, symbols of Wall Street's success in the second half of the twentieth century."[46]

The economy was in freefall by October. The Dow Jones dropped more than 20%, suffering its worst week of losses in its history.[47] Unemployment rates rose, and in an attempt to staunch the bleeding the government passed a massive bailout package totalling about $1,488 billion.[48]

We have yet to fully rebound from the housing bubble and the recession of 2008. It has been 14 years, and most stocks have not reclaimed their former peak levels. In comparison, it took more than 17 years for the dot-com bubble to return to its previous highs.

In reality, I think we're teetering on the brink of yet another tech bubble. The thing is, you never know you're in the middle of a bubble until the blood is in the water. But there are individuals and entities that not only weather such events, but thrive in them. Take our friend Warren Buffett—he managed to make money during the 2008 recession.[49] How did he do it?

The key is seeing the bubble forming before it pops. How do you do that and how do you invest properly when you suspect a bubble is forming? In the next chapter, we'll delve into how to recognize the early signs and make prudent investment decisions. It's the final (and possibly the most important) of my investing principles—risk management.

CHAPTER 13

WHEN I SAY RISK, YOU SAY MANAGEMENT:

Risk Management 101

"The elements of good trading are: (1) cutting losses, (2) cutting losses, and (3) cutting losses. If you can follow these three rules, you may have a chance."

— Ed Seykota

Close your eyes—I want you to picture something. You're buckling yourself into a rollercoaster, the anticipation and thrill coursing through your veins. The ride will be exhilarating, but lurking beneath the excitement is the ever-present knowledge that things could take a sudden and unexpected turn.

Investing can be a lot like a rollercoaster ride—a wild journey filled with ups and downs—sometimes you're hanging on for dear life and other times you're loving the ride.

Ups are part of the ride, but so are the very steep downs. Investing is the same way.

Let me be clear, I'm not here to spook you or induce undue panic. Rather, I share these insights—sometimes ones people don't want to hear—because thinking about what's around the bend is a vital aspect of effective risk management. My goal is to prepare you for the twists and turns that lie ahead, equip you with the knowledge and strategies needed to navigate the financial rollercoaster like a pro, and to enjoy the ride without losing your lunch.

In this chapter, we're diving deeper into risk management—a cornerstone of successful investing.

At Everglades, our core philosophy revolves around risk management. Our investment approach is meticulously designed to mitigate risk while focusing on companies with robust cash flows and high returns on invested capital. We love trying to find stocks that will do double duty: transform people's lives, but also avoid leading them to a financial precipice. We use price—among several other critical factors—to determine our entry and exit points, and we try to see around corners before good or bad things happen. I believe this is one of the key things that sets us apart from the others in our industry.

Our risk management strategy can be boiled down to two key practices.

1. We identify secular trends and recognize bubbles (before they burst).

2. We take appropriate actions to safeguard our investments or—put more plainly—take money off the table.

Simple? Yes, but much easier said than done.

As we've discussed, the market tends to move cyclically. There are good times and bad times, and they usually follow each other. This brings us back to our conversation about financial bubbles. Bubbles can be characterized as abnormal activity within a certain sector or asset class that disrupts the typical or natural rhythm of the market cycle. This disruption often results in rapid and unsustainable price increases—when the bubble bursts, this can lead to a sharp and significant decline in the affected asset's value. This sudden downturn contrasts with the stability that typically characterizes a healthy and well-functioning market environment.

Preeminent American economist Hyman Minsky theorized that "stability leads to instability. The more stable things become and the longer things are stable, the more unstable they will be when the crisis hits."[1] In other words, good times—a stable, healthy economy—allow for riskier behavior, which, in turn, makes crises worse if and when they happen.

Risk management keeps individual investors and the economy as a whole safer—although nothing is guaranteed, obviously. You might manage risk well enough, but you can't control the behavior of others. Your investments might tank before your eyes if you can't spot a downward spiral before it happens.

Recognizing bubbles is of significant importance because they are a regular occurrence in financial markets. So, how do you know a bubble is forming? Fortunately, bubbles follow a relatively simple blueprint.

The stages of a bubble are as follows:

1. **The New Frontier.** This generally occurs when investors are excited by a new technology, service, or asset—or there is fresh money in the market, possibly from lowered interest rates. James F. Royal, Ph.D. writes that bubble-prone sectors and assets are full of promises:

   "A compelling story is one of the best frameworks for creating a stock bubble. The dot-com bubble of the late 1990s had one: 'The internet changes everything.' The housing bubble of the 2000s had one: 'Real estate never declines in price.' Even the 19th century's railway mania promised that the massive benefits of the railroads would transform travel and transportation. These so-called story stocks promise to transform the world, and while the promised benefits may ultimately arrive, they tend to take a lot longer than the stock promoters would have you believe."[2]

2. **The Build.** In this phase, a buildup of anticipation and excitement gives investors the feeling of urgency that they need to invest ASAP and get in front of everyone else to make their millions. Often, media coverage amplifies this attraction and is excessive and exaggerated—this brings more people onto the playing field.[3] The fear of missing out (FOMO) can drive more people to invest, further inflating prices.

3. **The Fever.** The frenzy begins. With the publicity, everyone is on board. The entire world knows about this asset and is investing—possibly large sums of money. "When the taxi driver, the hair stylist and the grocery clerk are giving you investing tips, it's a good sign that an investment thesis has spilled over to the mainstream and is attracting less sophisticated retail traders looking for a buck."[4]

4. **The All-Time High.** As we've seen, the above excitement often causes a significant rise in the stock price and increases trading volume.[5] A major indication of a possible bubble forming is that prices tend to rise, even unimpeded by news that might ordinarily put investors off. As Royal puts it, "a company hits their earnings estimates? The stock climbs. And if it misses earnings estimates by a mile? It still climbs."[6]

Additionally, in a bubble the price often exceeds value. Value isn't an easy concept to pin down, as it is often relative to several other factors—these include demand, market sentiment, and even societal or cultural nuances. However, the price of a bubbling asset is often far and beyond "any rationally supportable construct of value."[7] In other words, if you really sat down and crunched the numbers, they wouldn't add up. An example of this would be the company's stock price being more than their expected earnings. (We'll hear more about a major company with that exact issue in a few pages.)

Regardless of signs of decline, frenzied investors in a bubble become convinced that the investment will never fail and often begin making riskier bets.[8] The money investors earn from the overvalued, bubbling asset shows up in other areas of the market, raising prices across the board.[9] This is especially true in easy money environments when interest rates are low. An example of this is collectibles—you'll often see them becoming quite a popular investment during a bubble.

This phenomenon is known as the Greater Fool Theory.[10] Investing in assets that don't turn a profit requires the investor to believe that someone else—a "greater fool"—will pay more for that Beanie Baby than he or she did originally. Investors disregard the actual value of their investment, convinced that they will make a return on it no matter what. The Greater Fool Theory tends to play out throughout a bubbling market—including with the hyped-up asset itself. The majority of investors believe that if things go downhill others will buy the asset off of them—regardless of the fundamental value of the asset, making the investment seemingly risk-free.

However, rising prices alone are not an indicator of a bubble. Just because a stock rises 80, 90, or even 100% does not mean that there is something amiss. That's why it's important to look at the price in context. In a bubble, valuations often reach extreme points, far beyond historical levels. Think real estate prices in 1980s Japan. Think internet companies tripling their values the day they go public.

At this point in a bubble, it's not uncommon to see certain people cashing in. They're the smart ones—we'll talk about them soon.

5. **The Crash.** As we saw in the previous chapter, seemingly minor events or triggers can make a bubble burst. Once that happens, there's no going

> back. As we saw with the Lehman Brothers, AIG, Fannie Mae, and Freddie Mac during the housing bubble of 2008, once the panic sets in, "asset prices reverse course and descend as rapidly as they had ascended.Investors and speculators, faced with margin calls and plunging values of their holdings, now want to liquidate at any price. As supply overwhelms demand, asset prices slide sharply."[11]

The smart people we talked about earlier make money—sometimes lots of money—out of a bubble. So, how do you do that?

First, you have to have a cool head and an objective eye. Warren Buffett made money amid the craziness of 2007 and 2008. He did that by avoiding the bubble entirely, looking for companies that were cheap with strong cash flows on the horizon. His composure allowed him to safeguard his money completely and add to his fortune.

It's easy to lose your sense of reality in the euphoria of a bubble, when times are good and money is flowing freely. The pre-bubble stage is lots of fun, to be sure. But that is exactly the time—as John Templeton would certainly tell you—to feed the ducks.

For those of you who are not familiar with industry jargon, "feeding the ducks" means taking some money off the table.

Once you've made a nice, respectable return on investment, cash out at least some of it. Protect some of the money you've made. Your portfolio might be up some crazy percentage, but that money isn't really yours until you take it home.

This is one of the hardest things I have to convince clients to do. When an investment has served someone well—especially for a long period of time—it's hard to let it go. It can become sentimental for people. I don't begrudge this, but at the same time, toxic investments can put an entire portfolio at risk. As I mentioned before, I always remind people that the country club is full of people who sold too early, but none who sold too late. Maybe it'll end up being the worst sale of your life—let's hope it is. That's much better than losing it all.

Even when a bubble is not part of the equation, there are times when you need to make tough choices like this. In general, when an investment has performed extremely well, it will become a very large part of your portfolio. That is the time to start exploring an exit strategy.

In 2011, we purchased a position in the Texas Pacific Land Trust, now known as Texas Pacific Land Corp (TPL). We held the stock from approximately $150 until it grew to $2,500. What started out as 3% of the portfolio grew to almost 50%. At that point, risk management and prudence took over. We sold some to cover our initial investment and then more on top of that.

I believe we're on the cusp of another tech bubble. But what makes me say that?

To start, the tech sector is bursting with good ideas—great ideas, even—that never really get off the ground. For every Apple, there's about a thousand rotten ones (get it?). Even if they do get off the ground, the likelihood that they'll become the next Microsoft, Google, or Amazon is becoming increasingly more difficult as the field becomes more and more crowded with players.

Truly novel ideas are few and far between. But when one comes around, it can reach dangerous levels. The excitement can grow out of control. Currently, we're seeing dot-com-level hysteria with AI companies, and many fear that we're in the middle of a bubble.

These past few years haven't been kind to the tech industry. Coming out of the pandemic, the tech industry has been groggily stumbling to a halt after years of non-stop boom. Then the economy took a downturn in response to rising interest rates, and big Silicon Valley companies—Alphabet (Google), Meta (Facebook), Microsoft, and Amazon—laid off thousands of workers. Stock prices fell and revenues slowed considerably. Tech was "one of the worst-performing sectors of 2022."[12]

But then, something new popped up onto the playing field—Artificial Intelligence (AI). With the ability to generate anything from complex code to ancient history, AI lit up the tech sector once again. Microsoft was one of the first to jump at investing in the newest technology catching everyone's attention. They made a "multiyear, multi-billion-dollar investment" in OpenAI, the company that brought the world ChatGPT.[13]

Bam. Just like that the AI frenzy began. Every major company raced to put out their own AI chatbots to compete with ChatGPT. Google, LinkedIn, Facebook—the list could go on forever—hustled to add new AI features to their platforms.

New start-ups began popping up everywhere, many of them AI-based. Investors ran to stake their claim in anything AI-based—"venture capitalists have poured billions of dollars into AI start-ups on spec, while in earnings calls over the past two weeks, tech CEOs have cited AI as a key growth area."[14]

AI has completely revitalized the slowing tech industry. Predictions have the sector hitting another 12 to 15% growth by the end of the year, "further boost[ing] investor sentiment," and "send[ing] the tech-heavy index [Nasdaq] to just shy of its all-time high of 15,971."[15] While on paper it might look like the Nasdaq is "just shy" of an "all-time high," other charts show us well above it.

You need to take a closer look, though.

In the last few years, many famed tech stocks have been moved into other categories.[16] It's not really clear why, but Meta and Alphabet were reclassified in 2018 as Communication Services from their original Information Technology classification. In March of 2023, PayPal, Visa, Mastercard, and Fiserv were moved over to Financials. Amazon, Tesla, and Netflix have been moved to the Consumer Discretionary and Communication column, respectively. If the above companies had not been reclassified, "the official IT sector weight today would be 37%."

In fact, if you add all the Information Technology companies back to their original place, the sector weight surpasses the dot-com bubble peak by leaps and bounds. Currently, we have the biggest consolidation of tech in the history of the S&P 500, even without putting major tech companies back where they were originally.

We might be in dangerous territory, especially with the extreme AI enthusiasm.

I'll explain—flip back a few pages to the stages of a bubble. Think about how many technology companies people regularly invest in simply because they're successful, well-known companies. Apple, Google, Amazon, Netflix, Tesla, Microsoft, and Facebook are some great examples. Although it's been a long time, I would classify this investment behavior as The Fever.

With AI making headlines, one could argue that we're reaching the All-Time High stage. With the frenzy around AI, the value of the industry has increased dramatically—

far above the dot-com bubble levels and far beyond other sectors. Since the tech sector takes up a huge portion of the S&P 500 (and other indexes) and the power is consolidated to a few major players, the entire industry is in an extremely precarious spot. "Bubbles form when a rising tide does not lift all boats. The concentration risk in what most people consider a 'diversified' market is very real, and very dangerous," *InvestorPlace* reported recently.[17]

As we said before, all it takes is one domino to fall for the rest to come crashing down. Imagine—a scandal makes headlines at Big Tech Company A and investors pull their money. Big Tech Company A crashes. Then Big Tech Company B—who had major holdings in A—collapses, facing billions in debt. Small Tech Company C—a project of B, fails as well—and the cycle continues.

It's hard to say what will cause the shoe to drop—or in this case, the domino to fall. The example above is an illustration to help you understand the highly-leveraged nature of the sector.

Because one of the most important questions remains—how will AI become profitable? Not only that, *when* will it become profitable? Generative AI technology is notoriously expensive to build and maintain, requiring "specialized chips, data server computing power, [and] expensive engineers."[18]

ChatGPT reached a milestone of 100 million users in a mere three months after its release to the public—but some reports are showing that use is already declining.[19] Not to mention that the tech is far from perfect. It routinely makes mistakes, passes off false information as true, and infringes on copyrights. Even still, start-ups of all kinds are "adding some kind of AI technology" to their business model, hoping that the magic lure of AI will bring more money in.[20]

Other consumer-forward tech—like social media platforms, for example—generate income from ads and data harvesting, and have relatively low overhead due to cheap access to cloud storage. Comparatively, AI is ridiculously expensive software that doesn't have easy income channels to push it mainstream or make it less of a financial burden on small start-ups promoting it to get investors.

Meanwhile, "tech CEOs repeatedly cite the value of generative AI to their businesses during earnings calls over the past two weeks, [but] there are still few details on how they will turn it into its own multibillion-dollar financial success."[21]

Is it all just hype, or will there be money in AI? It's not clear. What is clear, though, is that while AI has proven itself to be a powerful technology with much potential, it hasn't proven itself profitable—yet.

In the background is something a little more unsettling. Take Apple, for example. Currently, Apple's stock price is 29 times greater than its expected 2024 earnings.[22] One might consider buying stock in such a company if it was realistically meeting its 13% projected growth rate year over year, but that's not likely—at least not for the long-term.

That's because Apple is limited—"Even if Apple were a monopoly, only 63% of the global population have internet access, so it can't sell to every person." Furthermore, "securing sales from the remaining third of the global population—the 2.8 billion people without internet access—is unlikely to be very profitable, even if network access could be achieved, unlikely as that is. The disposable incomes, if any, of this 'untapped' population, must be exceedingly low."[23]

This doesn't factor in the other major personal technology companies competing against it—Samsung, Google, Microsoft, and Huwawei, to name a few. To meaningfully gain more business, Apple will have to win over some of the competition's business—but there's very little indication that such a thing is occurring.

Over the last few years, Apple has been slimming down its spending on equipment, factories, and other buildings, which shows that they are not investing in expansion.

Unfortunately, they're not the only company in that situation. Microsoft is also slimming down and slowing down, just in a slightly different way. Microsoft has been spending quite a lot of money on building data centers for its Cloud services, but the costs of those investments are rising faster than the returns. However, "earnings expected for 2024, at $82 billion, would be a spectacular 100% marginal return on investment."[24]

Both companies have also lowered their depreciation expenses—the cost of repairing or replacing assets such as equipment—in their accounting books, suggesting that their equipment will last longer before needing to be replaced.

Correct me if I'm wrong, but a fridge from the 50s can last longer than a fridge built yesterday. In most cases, technology built today is not built to last due to intentional technological obsolescence practices.

Why are they doing this? They're both giants in an "industry dependent upon product enhancements and new product cycles." What is the purpose of artificially stretching the depreciation of their assets?

They're not the only ones to do it, either. Meta and Alphabet "both revised the useful lives of their servers upward. This added nearly $1 billion of pre-tax profits for Meta and is expected to add $3.4 billion for Alphabet in 2023."[25]

Aha! There's your answer—making their equipment last longer (on paper) creates a form of return.

So, why aren't they investing in themselves more? It's possibly because their opportunities for growth are not very appealing. You might infer from this information that these massive companies are in the beginning of a very large decline.

To be fair, there are lots of factors to consider in massive companies like these, and there might be some information we're missing here. But the overall picture is rather concerning. Combined, these companies—specifically Apple, Microsoft, Amazon, NVIDIA, Alphabet, Meta, and Tesla—are valued at $11 trillion. Together they make up 27.6% of the S&P 500. Their combined revenue outstrips the GDP of most countries. Their forecasted earnings are high, and one might assume that they should be growing at rapid rates.

But that's just not the case. "For four of the seven, earnings were lower in the first quarter of this year than last year's first quarter. Of the three positive results, Microsoft's earnings were up only 9.4%."[26]

Nobody's paying attention to the warning signs, either. Investment in these companies is still incredibly strong, as their stock price performance had "an equal-weighted average over 81%," as of this summer.[27]

It's probably time to manage your risk and feed the ducks, my friends.

CHAPTER 14

CONCLUSION

"Taking risks today for tomorrow's reward is both the most challenging and difficult of tasks. Unbridled optimism must be tempered with reality."

— Sam Zell

A book like this is hard to draw to a close. Even as I write this, there is more relevant, updated information to talk about—more breaking news that underscores my philosophy and predictions. Forgive me for not including all of it. The financial world never sleeps, even though it might be nice if it took a nap once in a while.

However, just because this book will become outdated the second it's published doesn't mean it doesn't hold some crucial general advice for investors, big and small.

The crux of my message—time and time again—has been to protect yourself and your capital in any way you can. You do that by thinking critically, being adaptable, staying patient, getting creative, diversifying your portfolio, and managing risk.

As we've discussed several times—good times follow bad

times. Although the markets seem rather shaky right now, they will stabilize in the future. The market has a well-established history of rebounding that I have confidence in—and you should, too. But keep in mind that doesn't mean that things won't get worse or that poor decisions won't lead to ruin.

Even though the near future seems unclear, shying away from risk isn't the answer.

The key is to think differently. Whatever the masses are doing, wherever the tidal wave is sweeping, try to go against it. Just to see that it can't hurt. We mentioned that "inflation is indiscriminate, remorseless and without mercy," so you might as well peek at what's on the other side.

You don't have to put your money there, but you should at least attempt to think clearly about both sides of Wall Street—the popular side and the unpopular side. The frenzy and the forgotten. (As the famous Warren Buffett quote goes, "Only when the tide goes out do you discover who's been swimming naked.")

The truth is that thinking differently—taking the contrarian approach, thinking like an investor, critically thinking, whatever you want to call it—often feels uncomfortably precarious. Swallowing the inherent discomfort of going against the crowd and taking a risk can reap amazing rewards, as long as the risk is carefully managed. You can't—and shouldn't—take risks that are not appropriate for the expected returns.

Of course, the concept of risk itself is highly subjective. Your idea of risk will depend on your age, income, financial needs, and several other factors. While I encourage risk, I also encourage a healthy dose of objectivity. Risk management keeps the worst at bay when the financial waters get choppy, and they are definitely showing signs of getting choppy.

I digress.

As we speak, interest rates are climbing for the first time in nearly 30 years and bonds are in a 3-year slump. Coupled with our gaping national debt and massive tech sector being on thin ice, these issues are extraordinarily unprecedented. We have never seen such a market, and no one really knows how to invest in times like these.

So, what will you do? How will you handle whatever comes next?

Perhaps you'll follow my advice. Maybe you'll decide it's not for you. Perhaps you'll utilize some of it and discard the rest. Frankly, I don't care. You know as well as I do that my philosophies and strategies are not the key to success. There are many ways to invest, and no one way is best. As we've seen, there are many famed economists and investors who looked at the market with different eyes and different opinions, but all were successful. Ultimately, investing is a combination of art, science, skill, instinct, and sometimes a little dumb luck.

As I mentioned in the introduction, everyone should

be an investor. I'd like to add to that—everyone should be a capable, rational investor. There are too many things at stake to risk not keeping in good financial shape. Investing is a practice, just like everything else. The more you practice, the better you get.

After 40+ years of practice, my asset protection strategy in these unprecedented times is to use the investment principles outlined previously with a particular focus on risk management. I also recommend focusing on high-quality companies with good future cash flows and pragmatic, visionary management. Although those investments are generally not very sexy, they are reliable ways to make a return on invested capital.

However, my perspective is just one of many—like I said, you can certainly take another path and still find success. Regardless, it is my hope that this book has given you a new way to look at your investment decisions and your portfolio, protecting yourself and your future from the inevitable ebbs and flows of the market.

GLOSSARY

ARBITRAGE (p.26): Strategy employed in finance and investing to take advantage of price discrepancies in different markets or securities. It involves buying an asset at a lower price in one market and simultaneously selling it at a higher price in another market to make a profit from the price differential.

BANK PANIC (p.11): A financial crisis that occurs when customers withdraw their deposits from banks in large numbers, typically due to a loss of confidence in the banking system.

BERNIE MADOFF (p.16): Bernard Madoff was an American financier and former chairman of the Nasdaq stock exchange. He orchestrated one of the largest and most infamous Ponzi schemes in history.

BITCOIN (p.91): The first and most well-known cryptocurrency, created in 2009.

BLOCKCHAIN (p.92): A distributed, decentralized digital ledger that records transactions in a secure and transparent way.

BONDS (p.7): Debt instruments where investors lend money to a company or government in exchange for regular interest payments and the return of the principal amount at maturity.

BOND OFFERING (p.48): The process of issuing bonds by a company, government, or other entity to raise capital or borrow money from investors. The bond issuer receives funds from bondholders who are entitled to periodic interest payments and the return of principal at maturity.

BOND YIELDS (p.71): The annual rate of return an investor realizes from a bond, based on its face value and coupon.

CAPITAL (p.25): Financial resources or assets—including cash, investments, property, or equipment—that are available for use in business operations or investment activities. It represents the wealth or value that can be used to generate income or create additional assets.

CENTRAL AUTHORITY (p.95): An entity that has control over a system or network, often with the ability to make decisions and enforce rules.

CENTRAL BANK (p.1): An institution responsible for overseeing the monetary system and regulating the money supply.

COLD WALLET (p.101): A physical device or offline storage that securely stores cryptocurrencies offline, protecting them from potential cyber threats.

COMPOUND INTEREST (p.17): The process of earning interest on both the initial investment and the accumulated interest from previous periods, resulting in exponential growth over time.

COMPOUNDING RATE (p.78): The frequency at which interest is added to the investment, such as annually, quarterly, monthly, daily, or continuously.

CONSENSUS MECHANISM (p.96): The process by which multiple nodes in a blockchain network agree on the validity of transactions and the state of the ledger.

CONTRARIAN APPROACH (p.86): An investment strategy that involves going against prevailing market sentiment and making decisions that differ from the consensus.

CRYPTOCURRENCY (p.91): A digital asset that uses cryptography to secure transactions and control the creation of new units, often used as a medium of exchange.

CRYPTOGRAPHY (p.93): The practice of secure communication that uses mathematical techniques to protect information from unauthorized access or alteration.

DIGITAL WALLET (p.101): A software-based wallet that allows users to store, send, and receive cryptocurrencies.

EXIT STRATEGY (p.108): A plan outlining how an investor intends to sell or liquidate their investment in the future.

FEDERAL DEPOSIT INSURANCE CORPORATION (FDIC) (p.73): An independent agency of the U.S. government that provides deposit insurance to depositors in U.S. banks in case of bank failure.

FEDERAL RESERVE (p.8): The central banking system of the United States, responsible for conducting monetary policy, supervising and regulating banks, and maintaining stability in the financial system.

FEEDER FUNDS (p.31): Investment vehicles that pool investor capital and direct it into a larger master.

FINANCIAL COVENANT (p.1): An implicit or explicit promise or obligation by the government to manage its finances and economic policies in a way that promotes the well-being and prosperity of its citizens.

FISCAL STIMULUS (p.2): A government policy that involves increasing public spending or cutting taxes to boost economic activity during a downturn.

FRONT RUNNING (p.33): The illegal practice of a broker or trader executing orders on a security for its own account while taking advantage of advance knowledge of pending orders from its customers.

GOVERNMENT BONDS (p.68): Bonds issued by the government to fund social programs, infrastructure projects, or war efforts. They have little risk and provide stable returns.

GROSS DOMESTIC PRODUCT (GDP) (p.3): The total value of goods and services produced within a country's borders over a specified period of time, often used as a measure of economic activity.

HEDGE FUND (p.24): An investment fund that pools capital from accredited individuals or institutional investors and uses various investment strategies to generate high returns.

HOT WALLET (p.101): A digital wallet connected to the internet, enabling easy access to cryptocurrencies.

IMMUTABLE RECORD (p.94): A record that cannot be changed or altered once it has been recorded on a blockchain network.

INFLATIONARY MONETARY POLICIES (p.102): Actions taken by central banks to increase the money supply, which can lead to a decrease in the purchasing power of currency.

INTERNATIONAL REPLY COUPONS (IRCS) (p.25): Vouchers issued by the Universal Postal Union that allow the recipient to mail a letter or package without additional postage costs. They are used for international correspondence and facilitate the payment of return postage.

INTRINSIC VALUE (p.84): The perceived or calculated underlying worth of an asset or security, independent of its market price.

INVESTMENT ADVISOR (p.30): A professional who provides advice and guidance on investment decisions to individuals or institutions.

LEDGER (p.93): A record-keeping system that tracks transactions and balances in a financial system.

LENDER OF LAST RESORT (p.11): A financial institution that provides loans to other banks or financial institutions that are experiencing financial difficulties.

MARKET CAP (p50): Short for market capitalization, it is the total value of a company's outstanding shares of stock in the stock market. Market cap is calculated by multiplying the current stock price by the total number of shares outstanding and is used to gauge the size and relative value of a company.

MARKET DEMAND (p.49): The total amount or level of consumer desire or need for a specific product or service within a given market. It reflects the quantity of goods or services that consumers are willing and able to purchase at various price points.

MARKET-MAKER (p.33): A financial institution or individual that facilitates trading in financial securities by providing liquidity to the market. Market-makers ensure that there is always a buyer or seller for a particular security and help maintain an orderly and efficient market.

MARKET TIMING (p.88): The practice of trying to predict the future movements of the financial markets to make investment decisions, which can be challenging and often unreliable.

MARKET VALUE (p.44): The current worth or price at which an asset, investment, or security can be bought or sold in the open market. It is determined by various factors such as supply and demand, investor sentiment, and fundamental analysis.

MATURITY DATE (p.69): The date on which a bond becomes due and the principal amount is returned to the bondholder.

MINERS (p.94): Individuals or organizations that use their computing power to verify transactions on a blockchain network and add new blocks to the chain in exchange for rewards.

MONETARY POLICY (p.2): The actions taken by a central bank to control the supply of money and credit in an economy, often through interest rate adjustments or other policy tools.

NODES (p94): Individual computers or devices that participate in a blockchain network and maintain a copy of the ledger.

OPEN SOURCE CODE (p.96): Computer code that is publicly accessible, can be viewed, modified, and shared by anyone.

POLITICAL INSTABILITY (p.1): A situation where a government or political system is experiencing significant turmoil or uncertainty, potentially leading to social unrest or other negative outcomes.

PONZI SCHEME (p.24): A fraudulent investment scheme in which early investors are paid with funds contributed by later investors.

PREMIUM TO PAR (p.71): Selling a bond on the secondary market for a price higher than its face value.

PROOF OF WORK (p.94): A consensus mechanism used in some blockchain networks, where nodes compete to solve complex mathematical problems to verify transactions and add new blocks to the chain.

QUANTITATIVE EASING (p.2): A monetary policy tool where a central bank buys government bonds or other securities to increase the money supply and stimulate the economy.

RISK TOLERANCE (p.88): An individual's ability to handle and accept financial risk and volatility in investment decisions.

RUNAWAY INFLATION (p.4): A situation where inflation rates are increasing at an accelerating rate, potentially leading to hyperinflation or other negative economic outcomes.

SANCTIONS (p.4): Actions taken by one country or group of countries to restrict trade or other economic activity with another country, often used as a political tool to influence behavior.

SECURITIES AND EXCHANGE COMMISSION (SEC) (p.39): The U.S. government agency responsible for regulating and overseeing the securities industry.

SEC INVESTIGATION (p.33): The process of examining and scrutinizing potential violations of securities laws by individuals or entities under the jurisdiction of the Securities and Exchange Commission.

SECONDARY MARKET (p.70): A market where bonds can be bought or sold after their initial issuance by the government. Prices in the secondary market may differ from the face value or the amount originally loaned.

THE GREAT INFLATION (p.5): A period of high inflation in the United States during the 1970s, often attributed to factors such as rising energy costs and loose monetary policy.

TOKENS (p.93): Digital assets that represent ownership or access to a particular blockchain-based project or network.

TREASURY BONDS (T-BONDS) (p.72): Long-term bonds issued by the U.S. government with a fixed interest rate.

VOLATILITY (p.87): A statistical measure of the dispersion of returns for a given security or market index. Volatility is often used as a measure of risk and uncertainty in financial markets.

NOTES

CHAPTER 1

1. U.S. Department of the Treasury. (2023). America's Finance Guide: National Debt. https://fiscaldata.treasury.gov/americas-finance-guide/national-debt/
2. Congressional Budget Office. *The Budget and Economic Outlook: 2018 to 2028.* (2018, April 9). https://www.cbo.gov/publication/53651
3. Pew Research Center. (2023, February 14). Facts About the U.S. National Debt. https://www.pewresearch.org/short-reads/2023/02/14/facts-about-the-us-national-debt/
4. Peter G. Peterson Foundation. (2023) The Fiscal and Economic Challenge. https://www.pgpf.org/the-fiscal-and-economic-challenge/fiscal-and-economic-impact
5. This figure was calculated by taking the current national debt (at time of writing) and dividing by total number of US taxpayers in 2022.
6. U.S. Inflation Calculator. (Accessed March 2023). Current Inflation Rates. https://www.usinflationcalculator.com/inflation/current-inflation-rates/
7. Federal Reserve Bank of Dallas. *The Russian oil supply shock of 2022.* (n.d.). https://www.dallasfed.org/research/economics/2022/0322

CHAPTER 2

1. U.S. Congressional Budget Office. (2023, July 1). Major Recurring Reports. https://www.cbo.gov/about/products/major-recurring-reports
2. Goodwin, N., Harris, J. M., Nelson, J. A., Roach, B., & Torras, M. (2015). Macroeconomic issues and applications. The financial crisis and the great recession. *Macroeconomics in Context*, 371–390. https://doi.org/10.4324/9781315702735-27
3. Investopedia. (2023, December 18). *2008 Recession: What It Was and What Caused It.* https://www.investopedia.com/terms/g/great-recession.asp
4. Saphir, A., & Schneider, H. (2020, September 16). Fed vows to keep interest rates near zero until inflation rises. *Reuters*. https://www.reuters.com/article/us-usa-fed/fed-vows-to-keep-interest-rates-near-zero-until-inflation-rises-idUSKBN2670IX/

5. Federal Reserve History. (n.d.). Panic of 1907. https://www.federalreservehistory.org/essays/panic-of-1907

6. U.S. Senate Committee on Appropriations. (2022, December 20). *Chairman Patrick Leahy (D-Vt.) releases fiscal year 2023 Omnibus Appropriations Bill.* https://www.appropriations.senate.gov/news/majority/chairman-patrick-leahy-d-vt-releases-fiscal-year-2023-omnibus-appropriations-bill

CHAPTER 4

1. When good greed goes bad and what to do about it. (n.d.). *Financial Times.* https://www.ft.com/content/2bf893c2-b111-11e4-831b-00144feab7de

2. Levine, T *Truth-Default Theory — Timothy R. Levine.* (n.d.). http://timothy-levine.squarespace.com/truth-default-theory

3. Getlen, L. (2019, September 14). This man has a BS detector so good it almost drove him nuts. *New York Post.* https://nypost.com/2019/09/14/meet-the-man-who-knew-bernie-madoff-was-a-fraud-since-the-90s/

CHAPTER 5

1. Crane, E. (2021, April 14). Bernie Madoff victims included billionaires, celebrities and even retirees. *Mail Online.* https://www.dailymail.co.uk/news/article-9471431/Bernie-Madoff-victims-included-billionaires-celebrities-retirees.html

2. Corporate Finance Institute. (2023). Bernie Madoff. https://corporatefinanceinstitute.com/resources/capital-markets/bernie-madoff

3. Chen, J. (2023, May 27). *Ponzi Schemes: Definition, Examples, and Origins.* Investopedia. https://www.investopedia.com/terms/p/ponzischeme.asp#toc-origins-of-the-ponzi-scheme

4. Darby, M. (2013, November 17). In Ponzi we trust. *Smithsonian Magazine.* https://www.smithsonianmag.com/history/in-ponzi-we-trust-64016168/

5. Ibid.

6. Weisman, S. (2020, August 12). The history of Ponzi schemes goes deeper than the man who gave them his name. *Time.* https://time.com/5877434/first-ponzi-scheme/

7. Bloomenthal, A. (2023, November 2). *What is arbitrage? Definition, example, and costs*. Investopedia. https://www.investopedia.com/ask/answers/what-is-arbitrage/#

8. Julien Chaumond. (n.d.). *The rise of Mr Ponzi*. Pnzi. https://pnzi.com/

9. Probasco, J. (2023, February 28). *Who was Charles Ponzi? What did he create?* Investopedia. https://www.investopedia.com/who-is-charles-ponzi-5216783

10. Wikipedia. (accessed May 2023). List of Ponzi Schemes. https://en.wikipedia.org/wiki/List_of_Ponzi_schemes

11. Hare, B., & Gerken, M. (2021, April 24). 8 of the most notorious Ponzi schemes in US history. *CNN*. https://www.cnn.com/2021/04/24/business/famous-ponzi-schemes-generation-hustle/index.html

12. Dillon, N. (2022, February 14). Actor gets 20 years in prison for running $650 million Hollywood Ponzi scheme. *Rolling Stone*. https://www.rollingstone.com/tv-movies/tv-movie-news/hollywood-ponzi-scheme-actor-zach-horwitz-sentenced-hbo-netflix-fraud-1299908/

13. The Editors of Encyclopedia Britannica. (2023, May 13). *Bernie Madoff | Biography, Ponzi scheme, & Facts*. Encyclopedia Britannica. https://www.britannica.com/biography/Bernie-Madoff

14. Murphy, C. B. (2023, May 5). *What are penny stocks?* Investopedia. https://www.investopedia.com/terms/p/pennystock.asp

15. Hayes, A. (2023, November 1). *Bernie Madoff: Who he was, how his ponzi scheme worked*. Investopedia. https://www.investopedia.com/terms/b/bernard-madoff.asp#toc-early-life-and-education

16. FRONTLINE PBS, Official. (2021, April 16). *The Madoff Affair (full documentary) | FRONTLINE* [Video]. YouTube. https://www.youtube.com/watch?v=-rH1Y66IwKvc

17. Hayes, A. (2023, November 1). *Bernie Madoff: Who he was, how his ponzi scheme worked*. Investopedia. https://www.investopedia.com/terms/b/bernard-madoff.asp#toc-early-life-and-education

18. CNN. (2013, March 11). Bernard Madoff Fast Facts. https://www.cnn.com/2013/03/11/us/bernard-madoff-fast-facts/index.html

19. FRONTLINE PBS, Official. (2021, April 16). The Madoff Affair (full documentary) | FRONTLINE [Video]. YouTube. https://www.youtube.com/watch?v=rH1Y66IwKvc

20. Ibid.

21. Ibid.

22. Ibid.

23. Ibid.

24. Ibid.

25. KRyS Global. *About the fund - Fairfield Sentry Ltd.* (2018, February 19). Fairfield Sentry Ltd. https://www.fairfieldsentry.com/about-the-fund/

26. Henriques, D. B. (2021, April 15). Bernie Madoff, architect of largest ponzi scheme in history, dead at 82. *The New York Times*. https://www.nytimes.com/2021/04/14/business/bernie-madoff-dead.html

27. FRONTLINE PBS, Official. (2021, April 16). The Madoff Affair (full documentary) | FRONTLINE [Video]. YouTube. https://www.youtube.com/watch?v=rH1Y66IwKvc

28. U.S. Securities and Exchange Commission. (n.d.). OIG-509. https://www.sec.gov/news/studies/2009/oig-509/exhibit-0293.pdf, page 11

29. 60 Minutes. (2021, April 14). 60 Minutes Archive: The man who figured out Madoff's Ponzi scheme [Video]. YouTube. https://www.youtube.com/watch?v=3wUJesUik5A

30. U.S. Securities and Exchange Commission. (n.d.). OIG-509. https://www.sec.gov/files/oig-509.pdf, page 20-21

31. U.S. Securities and Exchange Commission. (n.d.). OIG-509. https://www.sec.gov/news/studies/2009/oig-509/exhibit-0293.pdf, page 1

32. Woodie, A. (2017, January 29). *The IBMer who decoded Bernie Madoff's RPG - IT jungle*. IT Jungle. https://www.itjungle.com/2016/09/12/tfh091216-story01/

33. Chernow, R. (2009, March 16). Madoff and his models. *The New Yorker*. https://www.newyorker.com/magazine/2009/03/23/madoff-and-his-models

34. Hayes, A. (2023, November 1). *Bernie Madoff: Who he was, how his ponzi scheme worked*. Investopedia. https://www.investopedia.com/terms/b/bernard-madoff.asp#toc-early-life-and-education

35. CBS. (2011, March 1). Madoff: "I tried to give money back" [Video]. YouTube. https://www.youtube.com/watch?v=KfiIwg3a8io

36. Reuters. (2021, April 14). Bernard Madoff Quotes. https://www.reuters.com/business/bernard-madoff-quotes-2021-04-14/

37. Chernow, R. (2009, March 16). Madoff and his models. *The New Yorker*. https://www.newyorker.com/magazine/2009/03/23/madoff-and-his-models

38. Menza, K. (2022, June 16). How Bernie Madoff took his family down. *Town & Country*. https://www.townandcountrymag.com/society/money-and-power/a9656715/bernie-madoff-ponzi-scheme-scandal-story-and-aftermath/

39. ABC News. (2008, December 26). Victims of Madoff's Massive Ponzi Scheme. https://abcnews.go.com/Business/story?id=6521133&page=1

40. U.S. Securities and Exchange Commission. (n.d.). Spotlight on Post-Madoff Reforms. https://www.sec.gov/spotlight/secpostmadoffreforms.htm

41. Cornell University. (2017, July). Trust in Financial Markets Was Biggest Victim of Madoff Case. https://news.cornell.edu/stories/2017/07/trust-financial-markets-was-biggest-victim-madoff-case

42. Investor.gov. (n.d.). Protect Your Investments: Types of Fraud: Ponzi Scheme. https://www.investor.gov/protect-your-investments/fraud/types-fraud/ponzi-scheme

43. Portfolio.com. (2010, August 5). Weisel lost everything to Madoff. *CNBC*. https://www.cnbc.com/id/29428542

CHAPTER 6

1. Olito, F., & Bitter, A. (2023, April 24). Blockbuster: The rise and fall of the movie rental store, and what happened to the brand. *Business Insider*. https://www.businessinsider.com/rise-and-fall-of-blockbuster#david-cook-opened-the-first-blockbuster-in-1985-1

2. Bussler, F. (2021, December 15). How churn analysis could have saved Blockbuster - towards data science. *Medium*. https://towardsdatascience.com/how-churn-analysis-could-have-saved-blockbuster-552336ea78f0

3. Olito, F., & Bitter, A. (2023, April 24). Blockbuster: The rise and fall of the movie rental store, and what happened to the brand. *Business Insider*. https://www.businessinsider.com/rise-and-fall-of-blockbuster#david-cook-opened-the-first-blockbuster-in-1985-1

4. U.S. Securities and Exchange Commission. (n.d.). "List of subsidiaries of Blockbuster, Inc." https://www.sec.gov/Archives/edgar/data/1085734/000093066103001225/dex211.htmAdd

5. Davis, T. (n.d.). *A blockbuster failure: How an outdated business model destroyed a giant*. Legal Scholarship Repository: A Service of the Joel A. Katz Law Library. https://ir.law.utk.edu/utk_studlawbankruptcy/11/

6. Phillips, M., Ferdman, R. A. (2022, July 21). A brief, illustrated history of Blockbuster, which is closing the last of its US stores. *Quartz*. https://qz.com/144372/a-brief-illustrated-history-of-blockbuster-which-is-closing-the-last-of-its-us-stores

7. Ibid.

8. Rodriguez, A. (2022, July 20). Netflix was founded 20 years ago today because Reed Hastings was late returning a video. *Quartz*. https://qz.com/1062888/netflix-was-founded-20-years-ago-today-because-reed-hastings-was-late-a-returning-video

9. Zetlin, M. (2020, February 6). Blockbuster could have bought Netflix for $50 million, but the CEO thought it was a joke. *Inc.com*. https://www.inc.com/minda-zetlin/netflix-blockbuster-meeting-marc-randolph-reed-hastings-john-antioco.html

10. Ibid.

11. Hastings, R. (2020, September 9). *CEO Reed Hastings on how Netflix beat Blockbuster*. Marketplace. https://www.marketplace.org/2020/09/08/ceo-reed-hastings-on-how-netflix-beat-blockbuster/

12. Antioco, J. (2014, August 1). *How I Did It: Blockbuster's Former CEO on Sparring with an Activist Shareholder*. Harvard Business Review. https://hbr.org./2011/04/how-i-did-it-blockbusters-former-ceo-on-sparring-with-an-activist-shareholder

13. Bussler, F. (2021, December 15). How churn analysis could have saved Blockbuster - towards data science. *Medium*. https://towardsdatascience.com/how-churn-analysis-could-have-saved-blockbuster-552336ea78f0

14. Satell, G. (2014, September 6). A look back at why Blockbuster really failed and why it didn't have to. *Forbes*. https://www.forbes.com/sites/gregsatell/2014/09/05/a-look-back-at-why-blockbuster-really-failed-and-why-it-didnt-have-to/?sh=24f7676f1d64

15. Forbes. (2011, April 7). A timeline: the blockbuster life cycle. https://www.forbes.com/2010/05/18/blockbuster-netflix-coinstar-markets-bankruptcy-coinstar_slide.html?sh=3579b9e55464

16. Hicks, A. (2020, July 13). *From PDA to smartphone: The evolution of Palm*. Palm. https://palm.com/blogs/post/from-pda-to-smartphone-the-evolution-of-palm

17. Google. (n.d.). History of Dish Stocks. https://g.co/kgs/DCf2VJu

18. Sharma, R. (2022, December 2). *Why Google became Alphabet.* Investopedia. https://www.investopedia.com/articles/investing/081115/why-google-became-alphabet.asp

CHAPTER 7

1. Lithium South Development Corp. and Emerging Markets Consulting, LLC. (2021, April 14). Emerging markets report: Lithium could run out by 2025. *GlobeNewswire News Room.* https://www.globenewswire.com/news-release/2021/04/14/2209842/0/en/Emerging-Markets-Report-Lithium-Could-Run-out-by-2025.html

2. Kang, D. H., Chen, M., & Ogunseitan, O. A. (2013). Potential environmental and human health impacts of rechargeable lithium batteries in electronic waste. *Environmental Science & Technology*, *47*(10), 5495–5503. https://doi.org/10.1021/es400614y

3. Varanasi, A. (2022, March 2). *We need safer ways to recycle electric car and cellphone batteries.* Popular Science. https://www.popsci.com/energy/lithium-ion-batteries-recycling-fire/

4. Katwala, A. (2018, August 5). The spiralling environmental cost of our lithium battery addiction. *WIRED UK.* https://www.wired.co.uk/article/lithium-batteries-environment-impact

5. Kelechava, B. (2023, January 20). *Nuclear power – the most misunderstood source of energy.* The ANSI Blog. https://blog.ansi.org/nuclear-power-most-misunderstood-source/#gref

6. U.S. Department of Energy. (n.d.). Solar Cybersecurity Basics. https://www.energy.gov/eere/solar/solar-cybersecurity-basics

7. Choi, D., Wittig, T., & Kluever, B. M. (2020). An evaluation of bird and bat mortality at wind turbines in the Northeastern United States. *PLOS ONE*, *15*(8), e0238034. https://doi.org/10.1371/journal.pone.0238034

8. Levitan, D. (2014, April 28). *Why wave power has lagged far behind as energy source.* Yale E360. https://e360.yale.edu/features/why_wave_power_has_lagged_far_behind_as_energy_source

9. Peplow, M. (2023, March 25). *Solar panels face recycling challenge.* Chemical & Engineering News. https://cen.acs.org/environment/recycling/Solar-panels-face-recycling-challenge-photovoltaic-waste/100/i18

10. Business Insider. (2023, September 12). Climate change will definitely not end the world as we know it: Elon Musk shares views on climate crisis. https://www.businessinsider.in/sustainability/news/climate-change-will-definitely-not-end-the-world-as-we-know-it-elon-musk-shares-views-on-climate-crisis/articleshow/103593171.cms

11. U.S. Department of Energy. (n.d.). Data Centers.

12. U.S. Energy Information Administration. (n.d.). Oil and petroleum products. https://www.eia.gov/energyexplained/oil-and-petroleum-products/

13. EKT Interactive. (2023, April 25). What is petroleum? https://ektinteractive.com/what-is-petroleum/#

14. U.S. Energy Information Administration. (n.d.). Frequently asked questions: How much oil is in one barrel? https://www.eia.gov/tools/faqs/faq.php?id=33&t=6

15. Chevron El Segundo. (n.d.). What's in a barrel of oil? https://elsegundo.chevron.com/our-businesses/whats-in-a-barrel-of-oil

16. U.S. Department of Energy. (2019). Products made from oil and natural gas. https://www.energy.gov/sites/prod/files/2019/11/f68/Products%20Made%20From%20Oil%20and%20Natural%20Gas%20Infographic.pdf

17. Ritchie, H. (2023, October 9). *Energy production and consumption.* Our World in Data. https://ourworldindata.org/energy-production-consumption

18. Gordon, M., & Weber, M. (2021, October 6). Global energy demand to grow 47% by 2050, with oil still top source: US EIA. *S&P Global Commodity Insights.* https://www.spglobal.com/commodityinsights/en/market-insights/latest-news/oil/100621-global-energy-demand-to-grow-47-by-2050-with-oil-still-top-source-us-eia

19. American Petroleum Institute. (2023, August 11). Updating the SPR: America's Energy safety net. https://www.api.org/news-policy-and-issues/blog/2023/08/11/Updating-the-SPR-Americas-Energy-Safety-Net

20. YCharts. (n.d.). U.S. crude oil in the strategic petroleum reserve stocks. https://ycharts.com/indicators/us_ending_stocks_of_crude_oil_in_the_strategic_petroleum_reserve

CHAPTER 8

1. Cussen, M. (n.d.). A brief history of bond investing. *BondFunds.* http://bondfunds.com/education/a-brief-history-of-bond-investing/

2. Reed, L. W. (2022, May 21). How the United States conquered inflation following the Civil War. *Foundation for Economic Education.* https://fee.org/articles/how-the-united-states-conquered-inflation-following-the-civil-war/

3. Gilder Lehrman Institute of American History. (n.d.). Selling World War I: Buy Liberty Bonds (1917-1919). https://www.gilderlehrman.org/history-resources/spotlight-primary-source/selling-world-war-i-buy-liberty-bonds-1917-1919.

4. Chen, J. (2022, June 6). *Liberty Bonds: What They are, How They Work.* Investopedia. https://www.investopedia.com/terms/l/liberty-bond.asp

5. Sutch, B. R. (n.d.). *Liberty bonds.* Federal Reserve History. https://www.federalreservehistory.org/essays/liberty-bonds

6. Ibid.

7. Ibid.

8. Chen, J. (2022, June 6). *Liberty Bonds: What They are, How They Work.* Investopedia. https://www.investopedia.com/terms/l/liberty-bond.asp

9. The Wall Street Journal. (2023, April 24). How bond investing can still (Sometimes) fail | WSJ [Video]. YouTube. https://www.youtube.com/watch?v=s_sNySZ4MM

10. Investopedia. (2022, August 9). *The bond market: A look back.* https://www.investopedia.com/articles/06/centuryofbonds.asp#toc-an-unkind-century-for-bond-investors

11. Chen, J. (2023, July 1). *Government Bond: What it is, types, pros and cons.* Investopedia. https://www.investopedia.com/terms/g/government-bond.asp

12. U.S. Securities and Exchange Commission. (n.d.). Interest rate risk — when interest rates go up, prices of fixed-rate bonds fall. https://www.sec.gov/files/ib_interestraterisk.pdf

13. Son, H., Goswami, R., & Vanian, J. (2023, March 11). Here's how the second-biggest bank collapse in U.S. history happened in just 48 hours. *CNBC.* https://www.cnbc.com/2023/03/10/silicon-valley-bank-collapse-how-it-happened.html

14. University of Washington School of Law. (n.d.). The collapse of Silicon Valley Bank. https://www.law.uw.edu/news-events/news/2023/svb-collapse#:~:text=Over%20a%20period%20of%20just,after%20Washington%20Mutual's%20in%202008.

15. Reuters. (2023, March 10). What caused Silicon Valley Bank's failure? https://www.reuters.com/business/finance/what-caused-silicon-valley-banks-failure-2023-03-10/

16. Tellez, A. (2023, March 13). Coinbase, Circle, Paxos: here are the major firms with funds tied up in SVB and Signature Bank. *Forbes*. https://www.forbes.com/sites/anthonytellez/2023/03/13/coinbase-circle-paxos-here-are-the-major-firms-with-funds-tied-up-in-svb-and-signature-bank/?sh=48c833f64574

17. Peter G. Peterson Foundation. (2023). The federal government has borrowed trillions, but who owns all that debt? https://www.pgpf.org/blog/2023/05/the-federal-government-has-borrowed-trillions-but-who-owns-all-that-debt

18. Vanguard. (n.d.). Improved outlook for the 60/40. https://corporate.vanguard.com/content/corporatesite/us/en/corp/articles/improved-outlook-60-40.html#:~:text=The%20typical%2060%25%20stock%2F40,globally%20diversified%2060%2F40%20portfolio.

19. Finkle, T. A. (2013). Creativity, innovation and entrepreneurship: The case of H. Wayne Huizenga. *ResearchGate*. https://www.researchgate.net/publication/264786617_Creativity_Innovation_and_Entrepreneurship_The_Case_of_H_Wayne_Huizenga

20. Ibid.

21. Andreassi, G., & Treadway, T. (2018, March 23). H. Wayne Huizenga dies; billionaire gave millions to Treasure Coast and cancer charities. *Treasure Coast Newspapers*. https://www.tcpalm.com/story/news/local/florida/2018/03/23/h-wayne-huizenga-who-built-his-fortune-in-trash-dies-80/452845002/

CHAPTER 9

1. Fernando, J. (2023, May 18). *The power of compound Interest: Calculations and examples*. Investopedia. https://www.investopedia.com/terms/c/compound-interest.asp

2. Zweig, J. (2023, April 21). Picking a stock for the year 2048. *WSJ*. https://www.wsj.com/articles/picking-a-stock-for-the-year-2048-66d90e

3. Chen, J. (2023, April 30). *Risk Averse: What it means, investment choices and strategies*. Investopedia. https://www.investopedia.com/terms/r/riskaverse.asp#toc-advantages-and-disadvantages-of-being-risk-averse

4. Barber, B. M., Lee, Y., Liu, Y., & Odean, T. (2014). The cross-section of speculator skill: Evidence from day trading. *Journal of Financial Markets*, *18*, 1–24. https://doi.org/10.1016/j.finmar.2013.05.006

5. Groette, O. (2023, October 2). *Day trading statistics 2023: The shocking truth.* https://www.quantifiedstrategies.com/day-trading-statistics/

6. TimsFord411. (2023, November 27). The amazingly famous person from winchester, tn you've never heard of. https://www.timsford411.com/blog/the-amazingly-famous-person-from-winchester-tn-you-ve-never-heard-of

7. Hayes, A. (2023, September 1). *Value Investing Definition, How it works, strategies, risks*. Investopedia. https://www.investopedia.com/terms/v/valueinvesting.asp

8. John Templeton Foundation. (2023, August 17). About Sir John Templeton. https://www.templeton.org/about/sir-john

9. The Philanthropy Roundtable. (2023, January 12). John Templeton. https://www.philanthropyroundtable.org/hall-of-fame/john-templeton/

10. TimsFord411. (2023, November 27). The amazingly famous person from winchester, tn you've never heard of. https://www.timsford411.com/blog/the-amazingly-famous-person-from-winchester-tn-you-ve-never-heard-of

11. McFadden, R. D. (2008, July 18). Sir John M. Templeton, philanthropist, dies at 95. *The New York Times*. https://www.nytimes.com/2008/07/09/business/09templeton-cnd.html

12. Templeton, J. (n.d.). *16 rules for investment success: And for your family, house, tuition, retirement*. https://www.franklintempleton.com/forms-literature/download/TL-R16

13. Lake, R. (2023, November 22). *Buy low, sell high strategy: An investor's guide*. SoFi Learn. https://www.sofi.com/learn/content/buy-low-sell-high-investment-strategy/

14. Templeton, J. (n.d.). *16 rules for investment success: And for your family, house, tuition, retirement*. https://www.franklintempleton.com/forms-literature/download/TL-R16

15. Ibid.

16. Ibid.

17. Ibid.

CHAPTER 10

1. Satoshi Nakamoto Institute. *Bitcoin: A peer-to-peer electronic cash system*. (n.d.). https://nakamotoinstitute.org/bitcoin/

2. Bitcoin.org. (n.d.). How Bitcoin works. https://bitcoin.org/en/how-it-works

3. Hayes, A. (2023, December 15). *Blockchain facts: What is it, how it works, and how it can be used.* Investopedia. https://www.investopedia.com/terms/b/blockchain.asp

4. River Financial. (n.d.). What is Bitcoin core? https://river.com/learn/what-is-bitcoin-core/

5. Britannica. (n.d.). How was cryptocurrency invented? https://www.britannica.com/question/How-was-cryptocurrency-invented

6. Hayes, A. (2023, November 4). *Who is Satoshi Nakamoto?* Investopedia. https://www.investopedia.com/terms/s/satoshi-nakamoto.asp

7. Redman, J. (2021, October 27). *The many facts that indicate Bitcoin's Creator Satoshi Nakamoto won't ever come back.* Bitcoin News. https://news.bitcoin.com/the-many-facts-that-indicate-bitcoins-creator-satoshi-nakamoto-wont-ever-come-back/

8. Hayes, A. (2023, November 4). *Who is Satoshi Nakamoto?* Investopedia. https://www.investopedia.com/terms/s/satoshi-nakamoto.asp

9. River Financial. (n.d.). Can Bitcoin be hacked? https://river.com/learn/can-bitcoin-be-hacked/

10. Connecticut Department of Banking. (n.d.). Cryptocurrency risks. https://portal.ct.gov/DOB/Consumer/Consumer-Education/Cryptocurrency-Risks

CHAPTER 11

1. Boissoneault, L. (2018, April 25). A 1938 Nazi law forced Jews to register their Wealth—Making it easier to steal. *Smithsonian Magazine.* https://www.smithsonianmag.com/history/1938-nazi-law-forced-jews-register-their-wealth-making-it-easier-to-steal-180968894/

2. Rosenberg, E. (2023, November 6). *Who is Sam Bankman-Fried?* Investopedia. https://www.investopedia.com/who-is-sam-bankman-fried-6830274

3. Ibid.

4. Sigalos, M., & Rooney, K. (2022, November 10). Binance backs out of FTX rescue, leaving the crypto exchange on the brink of collapse. *CNBC.* https://www.cnbc.com/2022/11/09/binance-backs-out-of-ftx-rescue-leaving-the-crypto-exchange-on-the-brink-of-collapse.html

5. Hill, J. (2022, November 11). Sam Bankman-Fried resigns, seeks Chapter 11 for FTX, US Crypto Exchange, Alameda. *Bloomberg.com.* https://www.bloomberg.com/news/articles/2022-11-11/ftx-com-goes-bankrupt-in-stunning-reversal-for-crypto-exchange?sref=CIpmV6x8

6. Evans, B. (2022, November 10). Sam Bankman-Fried secretly transferred FTX customer funds to Alameda Research after his trading firm suffered losses in the spring, report says. *Markets Insider.* https://markets.businessinsider.com/news/currencies/ftx-crash-client-funds-alameda-binance-sbf-sec-cftc-probe-2022-11

7. Goldstein, M., Stevenson, A., Farrell, M., & Yaffe-Bellany, D. (2023, November 29). 'Look, I screwed up': Sam Bankman-Fried is challenged on the collapse of FTX. *The New York Times.* https://www.nytimes.com/2022/11/30/business/dealbook/ftx-almeda-research-sam-bankman-fried.html

8. SEC.gov. *SEC charges Samuel Bankman-Fried with defrauding investors in crypto asset trading platform FTX.* (2022, December 13). https://www.sec.gov/news/press-release/2022-219

9. Ibid.

10. Ibid.

11. Levy, A., & Sigalos, M. (2023, April 27). SEC's Gensler says "the law is clear" for crypto exchanges and that they must comply with regulators. *CNBC.* https://www.cnbc.com/2023/04/27/sec-chairman-gary-gensler-says-the-law-is-clear-for-crypto-exchanges.html

12. Adams, R., CPA. (n.d.). *Crypto tax forms.* TurboTax Tax Tips & Videos. https://turbotax.intuit.com/tax-tips/investments-and-taxes/crypto-tax-forms/L8tQmA-LU3

13. Richardson, B. G. (n.d.). *The Great Depression.* Federal Reserve History. https://www.federalreservehistory.org/essays/great-depression

CHAPTER 12

1. Oil and Energy Online. (n.d.). Major oil market crashes in history: The 1980s oil glut. https://oilandenergyonline.com/articles/all/major-oil-market-crashes-history

2. Graefe, B. L. (n.d.). *Oil shock of 1978–79.* Federal Reserve History. https://www.federalreservehistory.org/essays/oil-shock-of-1978-79

3. Livingston, A. (2020, May 26). Last time Texas oil prices plummeted, the fallout changed everything. *The Texas Tribune*. https://www.texastribune.org/2020/05/18/texas-oil-prices-1980s/

4. Parry, I., Portney, P., Harrington, W., & Gruenspecht, H. (2003). The economics of fuel economy standards. *Ideas.org*, 2. https://ideas.repec.org/p/rff/dpaper/dp-03-44.html

5. Hayes, A. (2023, June 13). *Dotcom Bubble definition*. Investopedia. https://www.investopedia.com/terms/d/dotcom-bubble.asp

6. Ibid.

7. Goldman Sachs. (n.d.). Goldman Sachs moments: The 2000 Dot-Com Bubble. https://www.goldmansachs.com/our-firm/history/moments/2000-dot-com-bubble.html

8. CFI Team. (2023, December 7). *Dotcom Bubble*. Corporate Finance Institute. https://corporatefinanceinstitute.com/resources/capital-markets/dotcom-bubble/

9. Hayes, A. (2023, June 13). *Dotcom Bubble definition*. Investopedia. https://www.investopedia.com/terms/d/dotcom-bubble.asp

10. CFI Team. (2023, December 7). *Dotcom Bubble*. Corporate Finance Institute. https://corporatefinanceinstitute.com/resources/capital-markets/dotcom-bubble/

11. United Nations Conference on Trade and Development & United Nations Economic Commission for Europe. (1998). *The Russian crisis*. UNCTAD. https://unctad.org/system/files/official-document/poirrsd002.en.pdf

12. Owen, D., & Robinson, D. O. (Eds.). (2003, September 9). *Russia rebounds*. https://www.imf.org/external/pubs/nft/2003/russia/index.htm

13. Hofman, D., Kozack, J., & Zakharova, D. (n.d.). Russia: Rising and falling with the price of oil. *How Emerging Europe Came Through the 2008/09 Crisis*, 193–204. https://www.elibrary.imf.org

14. Owen, D., & Robinson, D. O. (Eds.). (2003, September 9). *Russia rebounds*. https://www.imf.org/external/pubs/nft/2003/russia/index.htm

15. Economics Observatory. (2022, September 27). Russia's 1998 currency crisis: What lessons for today? https://www.economicsobservatory.com/russias-1998-currency-crisis-what-lessons-for-today

16. Hayes, A. (2021, May 4). *What was Long-Term Capital Management (LTCM) and what happened?* Investopedia. https://www.investopedia.com/terms/l/longtermcapital.asp

17. Goldman Sachs. (n.d.). Goldman Sachs moments: The 2000 Dot-Com Bubble. https://www.goldmansachs.com/our-firm/history/moments/2000-dot-com-bubble.html

18. Hayes, A. (2023, June 13). *Dotcom Bubble Definition*. Investopedia. https://www.investopedia.com/terms/d/dotcom-bubble.asp

19. Ibid.

20. Ibid.

21. United Nations Conference on Trade and Development & United Nations Economic Commission for Europe. (1998). *The Russian crisis*. UNCTAD. https://unctad.org/system/files/official-document/poirrsd002.en.pdf

22. Owen, D., & Robinson, D. O. (Eds.). (2003, September 9). *Russia rebounds*. https://www.imf.org/external/pubs/nft/2003/russia/index.htm

23. Ahrend, R. (2004). Russian industrial restructuring: Trends in productivity, competitiveness and comparative advantage. ideas.repec.org. https://ideas.repec.org/p/oec/ecoaaa/408-en.html

24. Owen, D., & Robinson, D. O. (Eds.). (2003, September 9). *Russia rebounds*. https://www.imf.org/external/pubs/nft/2003/russia/index.htm

25. Economics Observatory. (2022, September 27). Russia's 1998 currency crisis: What lessons for today? https://www.economicsobservatory.com/russias-1998-currency-crisis-what-lessons-for-today

26. Hayes, A. (2021, May 4). *What was Long-Term Capital Management (LTCM) and what happened?* Investopedia. https://www.investopedia.com/terms/l/longtermcapital.asp

27. Goldman Sachs. (n.d.). Goldman Sachs moments: The 2000 Dot-Com Bubble. https://www.goldmansachs.com/our-firm/history/moments/2000-dot-com-bubble.html

28. Hayes, A. (2021, May 4). *What was Long-Term Capital Management (LTCM) and what happened?* Investopedia. https://www.investopedia.com/terms/l/longtermcapital.asp

29. Ibid.

30. Ibid.

31. Ibid.

32. Goldman Sachs. (n.d.). Goldman Sachs moments: The 2000 Dot-Com Bubble. https://www.goldmansachs.com/our-firm/history/moments/2000-dot-com-bubble.html

33. Hayes, A. (2023, June 13). *Dotcom Bubble definition.* Investopedia. https://www.investopedia.com/terms/d/dotcom-bubble.asp

34. CFI Team. (2023, December 7). *Dotcom Bubble.* Corporate Finance Institute. https://corporatefinanceinstitute.com/resources/capital-markets/dotcom-bubble/

35. Goldman Sachs. (n.d.). Goldman Sachs Moments: The 2000 Dot-Com Bubble. https://www.goldmansachs.com/our-firm/history/moments/2000-dot-com-bubble.html

36. McBride, J. (2018, September 12). The U.S. financial crisis. *Council on Foreign Relations.* https://www.cfr.org/timeline/us-financial-crisis

37. Singh, M. (2023, December 18). *The 2007–2008 Financial Crisis in review.* Investopedia. http://investopedia.com/articles/economics/09/financial-crisis-review.asp

38. Financial Industry Regulatory Authority. (2021). 2021 FINRA's Examination and Risk Monitoring Program - Net Capital. https://www.finra.org/rules-guidance/guidance/reports/2021-finras-examination-and-risk-monitoring-program/net-capital

39. McBride, J. (2018, September 12). The U.S. financial crisis. *Council on Foreign Relations.* https://www.cfr.org/timeline/us-financial-crisis

40. Singh, M. (2023, December 18). *The 2007–2008 Financial Crisis in review.* Investopedia. http://investopedia.com/articles/economics/09/financial-crisis-review.asp

41. McBride, J. (2018, September 12). The U.S. financial crisis. *Council on Foreign Relations.* https://www.cfr.org/timeline/us-financial-crisis

42. Ibid.

43. Singh, M. (2023, December 18). *The 2007–2008 Financial Crisis in review.* Investopedia. http://investopedia.com/articles/economics/09/financial-crisis-review.asp

44. CFI Team. (2023, October 12). *Lehman Brothers.* Corporate Finance Institute. https://corporatefinanceinstitute.com/resources/capital-markets/lehman-brothers/

45. Singh, M. (2023, December 18). *The 2007–2008 Financial Crisis in review.* Investopedia. http://investopedia.com/articles/economics/09/financial-crisis-review.asp

46. McBride, J. (2018, September 12). The U.S. financial crisis. *Council on Foreign Relations.* https://www.cfr.org/timeline/us-financial-crisis

47. Ibid.

48. Singh, M. (2023, December 18). *The 2007–2008 Financial Crisis in review.* Investopedia. http://investopedia.com/articles/economics/09/financial-crisis-review.asp

49. Ibid.

CHAPTER 13

1. Ganti, A. (2022, July 27). *What is a Minsky Moment? Definition, causes, history, and examples.* Investopedia. https://www.investopedia.com/terms/m/minskymoment.asp

2. James Royal, Ph.D. (2022, February 16). *5 sure-fire signs of a stock market bubble.* Bankrate. https://www.bankrate.com/investing/signs-of-stock-market-bubble/

3. Segal, T. (2023, August 2). *5 stages of a bubble.* Investopedia. https://www.investopedia.com/articles/stocks/10/5-steps-of-a-bubble.asp

4. James Royal, Ph.D. (2022, February 16). *5 sure-fire signs of a stock market bubble.* Bankrate. https://www.bankrate.com/investing/signs-of-stock-market-bubble/

5. Segal, T. (2023, August 2). *5 stages of a bubble.* Investopedia. https://www.investopedia.com/articles/stocks/10/5-steps-of-a-bubble.asp

6. James Royal, Ph.D. (2022, February 16). *5 sure-fire signs of a stock market bubble.* Bankrate. https://www.bankrate.com/investing/signs-of-stock-market-bubble/

7. Rogers, S. (2022, November 30). *What is a Market Bubble and How Can You Recognize One?* FinMasters. https://finmasters.com/what-is-a-market-bubble-and-how-can-you-recognize-one/#gref

8. Segal, T. (2023, August 2). *5 stages of a bubble.* Investopedia. https://www.investopedia.com/articles/stocks/10/5-steps-of-a-bubble.asp

9. James Royal, Ph.D. (2022, February 16). *5 sure-fire signs of a stock market bubble.* Bankrate. https://www.bankrate.com/investing/signs-of-stock-market-bubble/

10. Hayes, A. (2021, May 7). *Greater fool Theory: What it means in investing, with examples.* Investopedia. https://www.investopedia.com/terms/g/greaterfooltheory.asp

11. Segal, T. (2023, August 2). *5 stages of a bubble.* Investopedia. https://www.investopedia.com/articles/stocks/10/5-steps-of-a-bubble.asp

12. Saul, D. (2023, July 11). Here's how much tech stocks could surge amid 'AI revolution'—But some warn "euphoria" is unsustainable. *Forbes*. https://www.forbes.com/sites/dereksaul/2023/07/11/heres-how-much-tech-stocks-could-surge-amid-ai-revolution-but-some-warn-euphoria-is-unsustainable/

13. Oremus, W. (2023, January 23). Microsoft confirms 'multibillion-dollar' investment in OpenAI. *Washington Post*. https://www.washingtonpost.com/technology/2023/01/21/microsoft-office-chatgpt-openai/

14. De Vynck, G. (2023, August 7). Every start-up is an AI company now. Bubble fears are growing. *Washington Post*. https://www.washingtonpost.com/technology/2023/08/05/ai-hype-bubble-chatgpt/

15. Saul, D. (2023, July 11). Here's how much tech stocks could surge amid 'AI revolution'—But some warn "euphoria" is unsustainable. *Forbes*. https://www.forbes.com/sites/dereksaul/2023/07/11/heres-how-much-tech-stocks-could-surge-amid-ai-revolution-but-some-warn-euphoria-is-unsustainable/?sh=190a45c62237

16. Horizon Kinetics. (2023). How to talk about the bubble in the room, or a complex long-term data set walks into a bar. *2nd Quarter Commentary*, 5–23. https://horizonkinetics.com/app/uploads/Q2-23-Commentary_FINAL.pdf

17. Gayed, M. A. (2023, September 8). Stock market crash alert: The tech bubble is bursting. *InvestorPlace*. https://investorplace.com/2023/09/stock-market-crash-alert-the-tech-bubble-is-bursting/

18. De Vynck, G. (2023, August 7). Every start-up is an AI company now. Bubble fears are growing. *Washington Post*.

19. Ibid.

20. De Vynck, G. (2023, August 7). Every start-up is an AI company now. Bubble fears are growing. *Washington Post*. https://www.washingtonpost.com/technology/2023/08/05/ai-hype-bubble-chatgpt/

21. De Vynck, G. (2023, July 7). ChatGPT loses users for first time, shaking faith in AI revolution. *Washington Post*. https://www.washingtonpost.com/technology/2023/07/07/chatgpt-users-decline-future-ai-openai/

22. De Vynck, G. (2023, August 7). Every start-up is an AI company now. Bubble fears are growing. *Washington Post*. https://www.washingtonpost.com/technology/2023/08/05/ai-hype-bubble-chatgpt/

23. Horizon Kinetics. (2023). How to talk about the bubble in the room, or a complex long-term data set walks into a bar. *2nd Quarter Commentary*, 5–23. https://horizonkinetics.com/app/uploads/Q2-23-Commentary_FINAL.pdf

24. Ibid.

25. Ibid.

26. Ibid.

27. Ibid.

ACKNOWLEDGEMENTS

This book was the work of multiple brilliant minds, all of whom deserve credit for their input.

My partners, Peter Lacey and Mitch Hirsch, supported the time I put into this and were willing to review even the messiest of drafts.

My wife, Cara, read each chapter and gave me her thoughts from an outsider's perspective, which I deeply appreciated.

My daughters, Brooke and Hallie, have been listening to investing stories about Bitcoin and Texas Pacific Land Corporation for years. They deserve a round of applause for putting up with me.

My father, Len Arnold, was a noted legal scholar, judge, and author of over 40 editions of New Jersey Criminal Practice and Procedure. Although he is no longer with us, his legacy inspired me to take on this project.

My clients and customers have put their trust in me to be a good steward of their capital. They have become my best friends and have taught me more about investing than all my years on Wall Street. This book is for them.

I want to help the next generation of investors by paying it forward. A part of this book's proceeds will go to mental health service causes in Broward County, Florida.

ACKNOWLEDGEMENTS

[illegible]

ABOUT THE AUTHOR

Ken Arnold currently serves as the Managing Director of Everglades Parkland Advisors and Everglades Global Advisors. He is also the co-General Partner of the Everglades Global Opportunities Fund LP, the Everglades Digital Asset Fund LP, and OA Digital Fund LP. He earned a B.S. in Economics from Cook College, Rutgers University in 1983.

Ken boasts a wealth of experience in the financial services industry, having spent over four decades honing his expertise. He has held positions at prestigious firms like Smith Barney and Wachovia Securities, and his tenure as General Partner for the Total Allocation Fund LP from 2006 to 2008 is a testament to his leadership and financial acumen.

In addition to his financial expertise, Ken finds fulfillment in educating his friends about the intricacies of capital markets, passionately sharing his knowledge in this field. Ken also believes that individual investors can gain a significant advantage over Wall Street in the coming decade, a feat that has yet to be attainable in years past.

Beyond his professional pursuits, Ken actively engages in community involvement. He was a former board member of the Jewish Federation of Broward County and chaired his local community's annual "Men's Night Out" event. Furthermore, he co-chaired the Community Campaign Celebration alongside the Jewish Federation of Broward County. Ken deeply cares about mental health initiatives in South Florida, believing that contributing to society is paramount for a great country.

Outside of his professional and community commitments, Ken has dedicated over 25 years to training in martial arts, achieving a black belt in Jeet Kune Do and also training Muay Thai, both under the guidance of his mentor and friend, the late Sifu Neil Cauliffe. When Ken isn't practicing martial arts, he can be found working out or refining his golf swing in sunny South Florida. He and his wife, Cara, currently reside in Parkland, Florida. The couple has two daughters, Brooke and Hallie.

Ken's philosophy can be summed up by saying, "Do what you say and say what you do." This principle guides his actions and interactions in both personal and professional contexts.

Ken greatly admires the late American author and patriot Vince Flynn, whose works resonate deeply with him.

Made in United States
North Haven, CT
10 November 2026

22088894R00108